The Human Quotient:
The Most Potent Force for Your Business Success

JoAnn Corley-Schwarzkopf

| Content Guide |

Section 1: Introduction………………………………………………. 1
Section 2: The Human Quotient Explained……………………….. 13
Section 3: Helping Leaders Develop Their Human Quotient…... 41
Section 4: The Human Quotient in Practice & Profits………….. 73
Section 5: Summary Information………………………………….. 102

| Your Page Notes |
(Note your favorite pages below)

ISBN-13: 978-1727730036 | ISBN-10: 1727730038

| Introduction |

Let's Restore Humanity To Business - Are You In?

A potent force lies deep within every actor in business...a force so strong it can fuel a vision, make or break a dream. It's a power so remarkable it conjures inventions that have changed the course of civilization as we know it.

This force is the human force - the human quotient in business.

It's time to shake off the burdensome, blinding corporatism that is robing us of the full exhilarating expression of this extraordinary force (yes, it can be that way sometimes!).

This force translated into work renders meaningful contributions to...creates value for those around us, *no matter the endeavor*. Whether concocting the next big tech thing or making bread that feeds the world, all work has value and should be honored and appreciated.

We come to work bringing that force, the most precious thing we have - manifested as our unique "human recourse". That resource -- our heart, mind, spirit. body and all that entails is ultimately who we are - the essence of our being.

And every day we each *decide* how and to what degree we'll offer those precious resources to another's dream or vision while hopefully serving our own. It is a delicate dance.

Great dancing, beautiful dancing, skilled dancing requires a partner -- a partner equally skilled with complimentary contributions, appreciative of the deliberate union.

This is really the experience of work, of business no matter the role. And yet for many it's tainted - diminished to a compulsory participation in a battle for survival fraught with skirmishes for dignity, respect and appreciation.

Work can be a continuous, gratifying validation of our customized contribution to an endeavor, rather than laced with looming threats to the very essence of our humanity.

Can you imagine -- going to work every day not knowing how you'll be treated?...not being paid respectfully while millions are derived from the most precious resources on the planet...and I'm not talking diamonds, but rather the mind, body, spirit of every employee - those are the diamonds

It's time for a business reset! As business leaders, it's time to reclaim and celebrate humanity and its contributions to our enterprises.

Our enterprises - their operations, processes and management - have become so formalized it can sometimes feel and be dehumanizing. The more formalized, the more disconnected we seem to become from common sense and natural ways of interacting and just being...to the point of the ridiculous. Even the function of Human Resources can sometimes feel less human.

And, as technology advances its way into utter dominates of every operational aspect of business, the value of our humanness seems to be subjugated to its rule.

The call of the hour for every business leader, in every aspect of business, is to consciously, intentionally hang onto, cling to our humanness -- it is life itself...and is in fact *the source* of our business success.

Great Management:
Be the reason they stay, not the reason they leave.

My Past Can Serve Your Present & Future Success

"I've been around the block a few times, so let me save you some time…and a bit of money along the way."

It's been quite a journey these past years since I hung out my shingle in 1998. In the early years, I had no idea the twists and turns the road would offer. However, during those years, my resolve to serve the human community in the context of business has been an ever-present partner and it's stronger than ever.

I've traveled delivering thousands of workshops and seminars through-out North America on a variety of professional development topics, speaking in every major U.S. city and state. They've taken me from Nova Scotia to Alaska, from Puerto Rico to Hawaii.

And, I've had so much fun expanding my services to other areas of the globe. I was one of the first North American Job/Career Coach Contributors for the Daily Telegraph-UK and I've had coaching clients from Costa Rico to United Arab Emirates.

I've been named to multiple lists for a number of years, most recently Top 30 Global HR Influencers, Top 50 Unstoppable Women in HR and the top 100 Octoleader list. I would have never dreamed to be named to any list let alone a list to which many business influencers I've admired for years appeared, such as Tom Peters, David Edelman or Judy Hsu of ABC News, Chicago.

I've been quoted and contributed to major media outlets, invited to be an IBM Influencer representing the Talent Management space, and invited to be a LinkedIn Learning subject matter expert course author and mostly recently appeared on the Top Global 500 Female HR Speakers list.

The duration and unique experiences that have come my way since these past 20 years, have exposed me to a variety of employees and leaders, their conditions and concerns. It's given me a ground floor and c-suite view of a variety of attitudes, philosophies, and practices surrounding how business (profit and non-profit) as well as government entities run and work with human resources, talent management and development related to operational and organizational success.

This scope of experience has shaped a very specific point of view and provided significant insight surrounding how to effectively manage talent to best grow a business that will consistently thrive. The business community has evolved in positive ways and in others, hardly at all.

For example, integrating human resource-talent management into business planning and strategy (though many give lip service to this) is still not very prevalent. For many companies, there still seems to be an unproductive separation between these 2 areas.

After 20 Years - The Business Now

I have to say, it's hard to comprehend I've witnessed and participated in almost 2 generations of business as a young professional and then as a business owner.

As it relates to my area of expertise, I have come to see all of human resource management, talent acquisition and development (which includes leadership and management) through the lens *of optimal business operations and growth*.

My view and service approach has become simple and "holistic". Why? Because we've drifted too far away from the point of having a business and employees in the first place and that is costing businesses - daily.

Here's what I mean with a few examples. Two of the most important components of a company's growth, leadership and human resources, have both evolved over the years into flourishing, *independent industries* generating millions of dollars a year and in my view taking precedence over and in some areas over-complicating simple, common sense business practices.

Whether it's industry lingo (e.g. employee engagement-ugh!) performance reviews, assessments, HRIS software, big data, apps, managers losing their ability to be human, or chasing the next big shinny quality in "leadership success", these independent industries have influenced many an HR novice and other key decision-makers in a way that has hampered business operations and robbed profits.

> I've seen these capture the attention of decision-makers to the point of distracting them from the fundamentals that *really matter* in successful business building.

Simple practices such as treating employees with dignity and respect, meaningful communication, having standards for how managers lead, do what's right by the customer, intentional culture building. These among others, are the fundamentals that keep a business...well... in business.

No sense investing in newfangled recruiting software when key leaders still refuse to provide adequate leadership/management development to competently manage that talent! And we know, and I've consistently observed, **whoever manages the talent, dictates the talent**.

Why have yearly engagement or employee surveys when bully bosses are protected rather than fired...makes my head hurt.

Leaders are confused over "which style" is best, how to deal with millennials, difficult employees, experiencing overwhelm and many have little training or support.

What's worse, those issues get abdicated to the human resource department (many who are inexperienced in their roles and have little knowledge of working with human behavior) to solve and then have to beg company leaders to support their efforts to address them. The buck gets passed and continually ignored.

Do a Google or Amazon search on leadership and see the volume of results and yet a new book every year is written on the hidden keys or the unspoken whatever of leadership success. Consider this, there is more *free* information on how to be a good leader or manager than ever before and still ineffective or worse abusive leaders and managers persistent. Why?

Well there is a sad reality I've had to come to terms with over the years -- some leaders do not care about their employee's experience and what it may be costing them.

But here's the good news – there are many who do….who care *a lot* and are building businesses that reflect that. And those are the leaders I get to work with.

They are in the trenches shaping cultures that attract and retain great talent, they "love the dirt", (one of Gary Vaynerchuk's challenges). They embrace the digging, weeding and feeding that it takes to construct companies that can and will consistently thrive.

These leaders know that leadership and culture are the bedrock of their businesses and with the appropriate attention will prepare their companies to be successfully responsive to the ever-changing marketplace.

They are also keenly attune to the dated, traditional approaches to management and leadership developed that have not worked and are eager to embrace fresh approaches to ensure results.

It's 2018 and now more than ever, to lead these days is frikin hard and it bothers me how elements of the leadership development industry glorifies or idolizes it. Leading can be exhausting, full of headaches, jeopardize your health piling on unimaginable stress. Yet it can also be exhilarating and highly rewarding if approached with the right mindset and knowledge base.

And that's what we have the privilege of doing…helping leaders successfully build businesses where everyone can thrive! In order to

> Collectively then, our mission is to help company leaders build strong sustainable businesses that thrive and to do so in a way that saves time, mitigates losses and increases profits efficiently, effectively and sustainably.

accomplish this, our *approach has become holistic*. We see every request for our services through the lens of the operation and organizational quality that leads to profits and fiscal responsibility, depending on the type of corporate entity.

We see an organization as an organism (or even an eco-system) - knowing that everything impacts everything else. We've discovered there are seen and unseen ripple effects through-out an organization – both profitable and not.

Our services have evolved as the needs of the business climate have evolved, always with an eye to offering what's most timely and relevant within the context of our mission. For example, as of this writing, we are creating a strategic partnership of experts to help our clients effectively deal with the surge in sexual harassment awareness.

So over the scope of my 20 years in business, here's what I now see as the pressing needs for most businesses and its' leaders.

> Businesses have a great need to *effectively integrate* the human aspect into their operations so that the intended strategy can be successfully executed.

> That means human resource management must be seen as business/operations management -- not as a stand-alone, separate "department" that is treated as an administrative afterthought.

I talk about this in my executive briefing Show Me the Money! Without doing this, profits are undermined and operations bogged down with "people problems".

This is our #1 goal and area of expertise…**because effective integration *is the most* significant challenge and deficiency in companies today**.

Fortunately, it's easy to quickly identify…just observe how leaders think and the subsequent decisions they make.

If this is something you believe is hampering your organization or if our approach or philosophy resonates with you, please contact us to learn how we can help. We offer a no-obligation assessment and strategy session.

Because I've been around the block a few times, allow me to save you a few trips...and some money (and headaches) along the way!

To my current and past clients, as well as friends and family who have supported me through-out this journey, I am forever grateful!

To your success!

JoAnn Corley - Founder, CEO

JCS Business Advisors (formerly The Human Sphere) | We help leaders integrate human behavior into successful business building and management.

"Let's put the human back in human resource."

Cutting the Learning Curve

I wanted this publication to not only give a professional update, but also share some insights I've gained through-out the years that, if applied, could immediately improve an operation.

Have you ever had the experience when you've learned something and then say to yourself, "If I'd only known…"

I would frequently be approached at a workshop I was conducting and multiple attendees would say exactly that… followed with …I would have…or …If I'd only known when…and they'd share what situation they would have applied the learning.

In my 20 years of consulting and many more as a growing professional …I've turned that sentiment into "what I wish all leaders knew" (and there's a list for managers in the back).

That desire comes from seeing the same costly mistakes made in working with the human aspect of an enterprise repeated over and over again.

My observations and sentiments have been expressed over the years in my writing and books (subscribe to my blog) www.joanncorleyspeaks.com. Similarly, you can view them on LinkedIn and other publications.

In brief, I'd like to share my most heartfelt findings and insights in the arena of leading and managing people and how that impacts operational performance and ultimately successful business building.

There is a summary at the end, but for now this is my overriding, most important advice:

1. **Learn to see your business through the lens of the human experience** and more specifically through the lens of your employees and your own humanity.

2. **Assess your operations** with what you discover – see your human resource literally. (We'll address this later).

3. **Learn the financial connection** between your employees' experiences (performance) at every level, every title and your business outcomes. (This is such a compelling need which I address in my executive briefing "Show Me The Money).

4. **See leadership development differently** – not as optional, but as a *business building imperative.*

5. "Culture eats strategy for lunch," originally quoted by management guru Peter Drucker and made famous by the president of Ford Motor Company, Mark Fields. After 20 years observing business – this is absolutely the truth! The quality of a company culture directly impacts profits. **Culture is the human infrastructure of your business.**

6. **Create a culture of mutual responsibility.** Don't put it all on the leaders. A tremendous amount of employee problems would literally disappear if leaders created cultures where employees are expected to be grown-ups, taking ownership not only of their work but their behavior and relationships with others. Without this, managers feel like parents rather than collaborative partners.

Almost all of the work I've done over the past years has brought me to this advice and what I consider critical to saving time and money in operating and building a business, running a non-for-profit or governmental agency. No matter the entity you run, I have a strong conviction about intentional *financial stewardship.*

I can honestly promise you that if these 6 were achieved, you and those you lead would experience radical, positive, profitable changes and would constructively influence all operational decisions and leadership actions going forward.

The Human Quotient in Business

I've been wanting to write this business brief for some time, and am finally able to do so. I have felt compelled to because I believe it is one of _the most important_ books you'll ever read to be an exceptionally effective leader, human resource professional or business owner.

Why do I say that? Because over the 20 plus years I've been in business, working with the leadership, management and human resource community, I've seen a significant deficit in knowledge regarding this topic.

This lack of knowledge continually leads to poor decisions that undermine and even sabotage _the very thing_ leaders want – to be highly competent professionals and business leaders that make a meaningful contribution to building profitable, successful businesses.

I also say what I say because I've discovered that what I'm going to share with you is not actively taught in business schools or in weekend executive certification programs.

Therefore, there is a persistent knowledge gap and the value of this book.

What to Expect
Since this book is written for _busy_ leaders, I decided to present the information like I have done several other briefs -- in book form, with exercises and places for recording notes. Use the Content Guide page to record your customized table of contents.

The information is simple, straightforward, actionable and will be presented in sections rather than chapters. The learning points will be clear and direct. You'll also find lots of definitions. I discovered long ago having those offer a refined understanding of a subject or concept.

My goal is for you to make _undeniable_ shifts in how you _think about, see and understand_ the human quotient in your business... and, for that understanding to directly and significantly impact how you lead and run your business going forward – in a way that can be measured, profitably.

Positive people power is the most important fuel for business building.

Section 2 | The Human Quotient Explained

"My experience having people follow me has taught me employees don't want to be led, but shown the paths to meaningful work, sense of community, integrity, respect for the work & inevitably they build a place where everyone can learn & grow..."
@BruceMctague
(..and don't want to leave)

Imagine for a moment...

a company's leadership whose highest intention
is to create a thriving business *and* an exceptional, quality work life for its employees.
And in doing so,
consistently modeled, fostered and championed
these qualities in individuals and the organizational culture to make it so.

Respect
Dignity
Trust
Grace
Focus
360 Collaboration
Truth by way of Constructive Candor
Healthy Conflict
Emotional, Psychological, Physical, Spiritual Safety
Inspiration
Encouragement
Appreciation
Humility
Creative problem solving
Innovative process improvement
Personal maturity & responsibility
Tough-minded
Healthy Tolerations
Talent Challenges
Agile
Responsive

These positive human qualities, *activate* and *amplify* the best of each employee and in doing so produce a high-performing, immensely satisfying, work environment, in which employees don't want to leave.

These conditions, maintained, produce and sustain a company that can continually thrive in all ways, no matter the market conditions.

| The Human Quotient |

Quotient defined:
Quotient is used when indicating the presence or degree of a characteristic in someone or something.

https://www.collinsdictionary.com/us/dictionary/english/quotient

We use this definition in 2 ways:
1) The presence and degree of the human factor in business
2) And similar to EQ, emotional intelligence quotient, the degree of knowledge, understanding and use of the human factor of a leader in their business. Every leader needs a high "human quotient" to maximize their company's potential.

1> The presence & degree of the Human Quotient in business

Humans makeup 100% of your business...starting with you. Humans run your business. **They are your business.** They are either executing your business plan as an employee or are the target of your business plan as a customer.

Humans make or break your business. So, if you want to build and run a successful business, you can't escape them. You can't ignore them and the truths of their experience in your business...**this is the human quotient.**

Vision + Strategy + Plans + Process + Resources ➔ RESULTS

What drives and determines the outcome of ALL of these?
Your HUMAN resource

This truth has created our twist and *literal view* of "human resources". Your human resource is the #1 most important resource in your business.

*Your human resources **is** your business!*

Definition part 2:

2> The Human Quotient: The degree of knowledge, understanding and use of the human factor as a leader. (*It's beyond EQ – it's HQ*).

Now all the points under #1 may sound utterly silly. Right? It's so obvious, why even state it! Stating it the way I did could feel downright insulting to any intelligent person.

And you know...you're absolutely right.

> Yet, many leaders do not behave as if this is true.
> Many of their decisions do not reflect so.

How do I know? In the work I've done and as I invite you to examine the many failures in business, the struggles, the challenges, the complaints, the unattended needs, you'll discover **they are all** human related in some way. Every failure, challenge or success can be simply traced to someone's thinking, feelings, decisions or behavior – the human quotient.

How we think, what we feel and the subsequent results comprise the human experience and its impact to your business.

Therefore, an *essential ingredient* in effective leadership, is being mindful of these human truths while running and building a business. It should be a critical reference point for every decision made.

The 4 Key Elements of the Human Quotient

Introduction

At the core of the human experience are thoughts and feelings.

As mentioned, every failure, challenge or success in business can be tied to someone's thinking, feelings, decisions or behavior.

More specifically, that means *all activities* related to business operations are <u>channeled through the human experience</u> of thinking and feeling which results in decisions and behaviors.

Let that sink in for a moment.

<u>Everything</u> you want to happen in your business is **funneled through** the thoughts and feelings of you and your employees.

Those thoughts and feelings produce results – the ones you want and *the ones you don't* want.

< Examples >

Example #1: You as the Owner or Leader
Need: Increased sales

Your thinking, "I want to improve my sales, but I have limited capital to work with. What if I spend the little I have and I don't get the results I need…where will the business be?"

This thinking or *thought* process could possibly generate the *feeling of fear* or determination or…

The feeling of fear potentially produces these results:
- Decision to not spend money
- Paralyzed action… the *behavior* (ability to act thwarted)
- The business slows or stops growing.

These 3 results suggest a chain of outcomes -- what we call **the ripple effect**. In most cases, the *subsequent results* of what we think and feel will produce results that create a ripple effect.

Leadership Reflection

Starter Questions…

__ Are you aware of your thinking and how it impacts your decisions?

__ Are you aware of your feelings and how they impact your decisions? Are you aware of the decisions and behaviors related to the business?

__ The same questions relates to fellow leaders, team members – aware of how they think?... what emotions influence their decisions?

Notes

Example #2: An Employee
Need: An employee needs to improve productivity to reach expected targets. The employee seems to be losing motivation as compared to past performance.

The employee is losing motivation because he/she *thinks*, "No matter how well I do, no one really cares." The feeling/thinking is... there is little meaningful recognition for hard work.

The resulting feelings could be sadness, discouragement, sense of loss related to worth or value... which are "demotivators".

Potential ripple effect: The attitude could be expressed to other team members, which if believed could impact their motivation, which would most likely impact productivity, or service to clients or customers.

Leadership Reflection

Think of and record a personal example of becoming demotivated or something similar as an employee or...a team member becoming so from a conversation you've had.

Starter Questions:
When have you been demotivated? What were you thinking...feeling? Why?
When has a team member been demotivated? Why?

Human Truths
Thinking generates feelings.
Feelings influence decisions & behavior
Feelings are energy, they fuel motivation and influence levels of motivation.
Meaningful recognition motivates.

Human Element #1: Our Thinking

Our thinking is derived by how our brain processes current and past experiences through our unique brain wiring.

Brain wiring and how it processes information has be popularly known as left-brain right brain. And though that is not literally how the brain "thinks", multiple areas of brain function at one time - when we think, there are specific characteristics or functions that have been attributed to each side. The chart below is a brief glimpse.

Left Brain	Right Brain
logic	Divergent thinker
reasoning	Open
analytical	Spontaneous
rational	Mystical
detailed	Intuitive
need for control	Imaginative
need to be right	Big picture
need to be correct	Multi-dimensional
linear – one thing at a time	general
convergent thinker	
precision	

Our thinking is also shaped and influenced by diverse sources of experiences:
- Family: culture, gender, birth order
- Natural Wiring: personality, left/right brain
- Social Development
  - Hobbies
  - Neighborhood
  - Spiritual
  - Schools
  - Regional
  - Country of origin
  - Generation
- Work Life
  - Jobs
  - Industry
  - Bosses
  - Company
- Acquired knowledge to date

From our unique life experience and brain wiring, we develop filters and a lens through which we interpret (give meaning to…try to make sense of) each life event. Our filters and lens produce a particular point of view or interpretation which can be called an unconscious bias. By the way, in its purest form, bias is not a bad thing – it is naturally created as we continually process our experiences.

This is why two people can have the exact same experience and interpret them completely different ways.

A Bit More About Our Lens
Our brains are like sponges. Even before we had a conscious memory, it absorbed and stored every nuanced detail of our life experience. Ever been irritated or angry for no reason?

Those meticulously recorded memories began to shape our values and beliefs and are deeply stored in our subconscious, and the emotions associated with them can be triggered or retrieved at any time. Triggers many times present a wanted *or unwanted* opportunity to recall a long forgotten event or group of emotions, which can cause reactions to present events or people for no logical reason.

I tell new managers that in many cases if someone is responding negatively to you, it's probably not about you, but something being triggered from a past experience or boss. Now in 6 months, it may be about you, because an experience has been formed from which current thinking and emotions have been created.

Unknowingly to many, all these "recordings" create a lens and filter which serves to make sense of and interpret new experiences as we move through life.

Also, of important note, they shape our *values* (what matters most) and our *beliefs* (what's true to you).

The lens and filter creates a customized, unconscious bias and sense of right and wrong which is used to assess or judge leading to a decision. That process of assessing and judging crafts an internal story that serves as the interpretation of the experience.

Our interpretation – known as perception - becomes the story we communicate to ourselves and others. It's typically a harmless, unconscious, biased perception.

This interpretation/perception then becomes our reality and our truth, sometimes regardless of whether it is rational or true to others.

That's why, two people can have the exact same experience and interpret it in completely different ways and this is where the source of potential conflict can begin.

The degree and level of conflict are dependent on *how we handle differing perceptions.* For example, we can choose to say someone else's perception is wrong and insist on ours being right, even vilifying the person with a differing viewpoint.

Or we can honor someone else's perception, not make it wrong, acknowledge that "it just is" and respect it accordingly – even though we might vehemently disagree. This takes a tremendous amount of emotional maturity!

Side Note – An Example of Beliefs
A leader decides that the action to take is to provide coaching to improve performance of a team member. When that action is taken although with the honorable intent is to be helpful, the employee may not experience or appropriately receive the coaching because there is a *belief* the manager really doesn't care *(continued from example #2, page 17).*

Expanded Bias
Of critical importance is to recognize that once our perception is formed, the brain becomes selective in what it sees ("zeros in on") going forward and how it interprets.

We have an innate need to have our world make sense to us because it defines our identity, self-worth, self-esteem, and our place in it. So our brain looks for ways to consistently secure and reinforce these by confirming and reinforcing previous interpretations.

This is called unconscious *confirmation* bias.

The more frequent and intense the confirmation, *the more right we feel* as values and beliefs are <u>cemented</u>.

Unconscious confirmation bias can greatly inhibit our ability to see an event or experience with a fresh, "clear lens" that is essential to our choosing a different path, making an uncomfortable decision or being open to new ideas.

It takes a **conscious awareness and effort** on our part to battle the bias or preconceived notions of a person, place or thing.

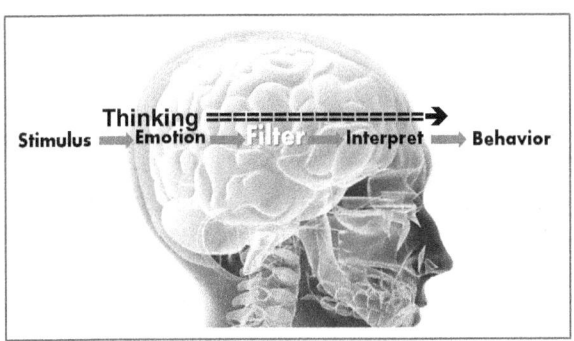

Human Truths
We all have a *unique lens* for our collective life experience.
We filter experiences differently.
We *look to confirm* what we already believe or know both consciously & subconsciously

Human Element #2: Feelings & Emotions
It's been said that there are only few base feelings/emotions from which all else are derived. And there is debate over how to define feelings and emotions, since many use these words interchangeably.

I won't go into great detail, and I don't what us to get hung up on slicing and dicing definitions. I'll provide a brief introduction here and some resource links for future study.

In short:
1. Emotions and feelings are both sensations experienced by humans.

2. Feelings are triggered by external stimuli whereas emotions come
3. Feelings can include physical sensations as well as mental states, but emotions always come from your mind.

Great examples:

"Experiencing Feelings and Emotions
Feelings are thought to be experienced for short periods of time. If you touch a stove it feels hot and you quickly remove your hand. Within minutes you are no longer feeling hot. If someone jumps out at you from around a corner you will feel startled, but that will soon pass. Feelings of excitement will subside after the awaited event is done.

Emotions are often said to be long-term states. If you are in love that emotion will usually last years. Sorrow too, takes a long time to go away. Because emotions are internal you have to change your mind set to change your emotion and this process takes time."

Source: http://www.differencebetween.net/miscellaneous/difference-between-feelings-and-emotions/#ixzz5SmfDSIXX

Emotions can been seen as the result of a feeling or even vice versa (same coin different side).

Going Forward
In the work we do with emotional intelligence, we talk about emotions and feelings and how to effectively manage them. And no matter what you call them – whatever term is most familiar to you – we initially identify them as **neutral energy** that is not to be judged.

Every feeling or emotion has an energy to it that fuels, drives or diminishes a behavior in some way – for the one expressing or experiencing it and even for the one experiencing it when evoked by someone else. For example: an act of kindness gives energy to the person expressing it and to the one receiving it.

If behavior produces outcomes, then being mindful of how leadership activity influences emotions is important.

To follow is a great chart of core feelings (which some identify as emotions) and how to leverage them in a positive way.

As you can see, feelings/emotions shape and define our life and therefore we need to pay attention to them and in particular how they are expressed and define our human experience in the context of business.

8 BASIC FEELINGS	HOW WE FEEL THEM	AND THEIR GIFTS
Anger	Resentment	Assertiveness
	Irritation	Strength
	Frustration	Energy
Fear	Apprehension	Preservation
	Overwhelmed	Wisdom
	Threatened	Protection
Pain	Hurt	Healing
	Pity	Growth
	Sad, Lonely	Awareness
Joy	Happy	Abundance
	Elated	Happiness
	Hopeful	Gratitude
Passion	Enthusiasm	Appetite
	Desire	Energy
	Zest	Excitement
Love	Affection, Warmth	Connection
	Tenderness	Life
	Compassion	Spirituality
Shame	Embarrassment	Humility
	Humble	Containment
	Exposed	Humanity
Guilt	Regretful	Values
	Contrite	Amends
	Remorseful	Containment

https://www.solutions-recovery.com/blog/the-8-core-emotions/
*Original chart info courtesy of Pia Mellody

Emotional Intelligence – Effective Emotion Management

"Because emotions are internal you have to change your mindset to change your emotion."

Taken from our referenced definition, we need to get a better sense of where emotions come from, how we *voluntarily* generate them and our ability to successfully work with and manage them.

This formula reflects a simplified explanation of the process when emotions are generated:

Event => Thinking / Trigger => Emotion => Decision => Behavior

Looking at this process, (which I use even for my own self coaching) we can see the chain reaction when experiencing a life event. What's important to note is that **thinking** (as well as triggers) **causes, creates emotions.**

So, your thinking, <u>how you describe</u> an event to yourself, will generate an emotion.

This is great to know, because we can in some ways manage our emotions by managing our thinking.

A great example of this is self-induced stress. If you tell yourself something is awful or overwhelming *you will begin to feel that way* – experience those emotions - and say to yourself. "I feel stressed…I feel overwhelmed."

Here's the kicker, the more you say it to yourself, the more intense and amplified the feeling becomes. …the bigger it all feels. Hence the phrase, "turning a mole hill into a mountain."

In fact if you think about something for an extended period time – beyond an initial thought – your thinking will create a picture or movie that your brain then responds to by stimulating chemicals and emotions - <u>whether the picture is true or not.</u>

Your mind does not distinguish between reality and fantasy. Here's a great acronym that reflects that:

F antsized
E vent
A ppearing
R real

So, thinking creates pictures and movies, which then generate feelings/emotions and releases chemicals that provide a sense of energy and well-being, calm or stress, low energy or motivation.

The 4 most popular chemicals that give **energy, sense of well-being, and happiness** are: dopamine, oxytocin, serotonin, endorphins.

This is where the term "toxic people" comes into play. Those who are toxic, for example habitually negative people, suppress the positive, energizing chemical and cause the release of chemicals (cortisol) that cause a sense of "depressed" energy, exhaustion or stress.

By the way, when I evaluate a team I consider their "chemistry' in the most literal sense. Is the *team dynamic producing* the kinds of positive chemicals that fuel motivation through a sense of good will, safety, trust, and well-being.

Here's a link to a useful article for further study: Hacking Into Your Happy Chemicals: Dopamine, Serotonin, Endorphins, & Oxytocin
http://theutopianlife.com/2014/10/14/hacking-into-your-happy-chemicals-dopamine-serotonin-endorphins-oxytocin/

The Leadership Effect – What Are You Activating?
Leaders can be drains or fountains…

So here's an invaluable conclusion we can draw: negative leadership behaviors can most likely produce negative emotional results and stressor hormones initially and going forward. In fact long term, those behaviors could create a "conditioned" pattern -- even to the point of consistently "depressing" motivation and energy.

Additionally, the latest neural science revealed in the work done by Dr. Daniel Goleman, who popularized Emotional Intelligence, suggests, that leaders are activating, influencing behavior and performances in ways not readily seen because leaders and followers are interconnected through mirror neurons."

"The salient discovery is that certain things leaders do—specifically, exhibit empathy and become attuned to others' moods—literally affect both their own brain chemistry and that of their followers. Indeed, researchers have found that the leader-follower dynamic is not a case of two (or more) independent brains reacting consciously or unconsciously to each other. Rather, the individual minds become, in a sense, fused into a single system.

*The notion that effective leadership is about having powerful social circuits in the brain has prompted us to extend our concept of emotional intelligence, which we had grounded in theories of individual psychology. A more relationship-based construct for assessing leadership is social intelligence, which we define as a set of interpersonal competencies built on specific neural circuits (and related endocrine systems) that **inspire** others to be effective."*

https://hbr.org/2008/09/social-intelligence-and-the-biology-of-leadership

> We substantially impact those we lead and work with, whether we want to or not...whether we *own it* or not!

And so, what Dr. Goleman advocates, as do we, is that effective leadership, in fact a leadership competency is understanding appropriate responses to the human experience – even down to the neural level. Dr. David Rock in his work calls it "neural leadership".

At the close of this section, we've left a good bit of room for reflections notes. Please take the time to digest and apply this to your company experiences.

Leadership Reflection: This would be a great time to take a moment to think about how emotions, emotional energy, feelings have impacted you, your team and your business in general. Building awareness, being able to recognize them is a critical element of a leaders' HQ, human quotient.

Notes

Human Truths
Feelings are fuel.
We are interconnected through our brains.

Human Element #3: Decisions

Decisions are conclusions resulting from what we think and the feelings/emotions generated from that thinking.

There are 4 general decision-making styles: decisive, spontaneous, methodical, inclusive. Most have a dominant style, however high-performing leaders are agile and appropriately responsive using all of them as a situation requires.

Using the same style for every situation is a sign of leadership/ management immaturity.

Related to decision-making is judgment. A judgment is defined as the ability to judge, make a decision, or form an opinion objectively, authoritatively, and wisely, especially in matters affecting action; good sense; discretion.

Also related – discernment… it's a critical capability in leadership. It's defined as: the faculty of discerning; discrimination; acuteness of judgment & understanding. Discern to be able to see, recognize, understand, or decide something.

All three of these: decisions, judgment and discernment are of paramount importance in effective leadership and therefore should be monitored and coached accordingly.

Here's an interesting tip: When considering several candidates for a promotion, one factor to examine is their decision-making (which is a reflection of judgment and discernment)…what is their natural style, look at the results of past decisions. You'll gain important clues to how they will lead and manage in the future.

Why is Decision-Making Such a Big Deal in Leadership?

- Decisions create results.
- Decisions prompt what we say and do.
- Decisions have a ripple effect.
- Decision impact money.

> When you think about building and/or running a business, <u>every single element</u> of it revolves around decisions.
>
> **Decisions are the building blocks of your business.**
> *or…could be the downfall.*

You could say then, that at the core of effective leadership and management is skilled decision-making.

The Role of Emotions
Think for a moment about the most common emotions that influence decisions. Here is a list of some of the more popular that have been comprised from my time management and emotional intelligence workshops through-out the years:

- Fear
- Anger
- Guilt (very popular)
- Love
- Satisfaction
- Competition
- Pleasure
- Pride
- Obligation
- Duty
- Tired
- Sadness
- Frustration
- Sympathy
- Irritation
- Caring, Concern

Side Note: Time management is really about decision management – <u>deciding</u> what to do with time.

Leadership Reflection: How have these or other emotions impacted your decision-making? What's your awareness regarding what influences your decision-making? If you don't have a keen awareness – chart if for 30 days. Look for patterns. What do you want to discover from this exercise. How can that impact your leadership effectiveness and business outcomes? Include in your reflections thoughts about judgement & discernment…important qualities in leadership.

Human Element #4: Behaviors – What We Say & Do

This element is the most obvious because we can see and directly experience its impact every day.

Leaders need to see beyond people, to their behaviors. Also, it's the behaviors that you want to develop and coach.

From a business management perspective, since behaviors have a direct financial impact, we see behaviors as profitable, unprofitable or neutral.

Leadership Reflection
This concept is so simple and yet is not readily acknowledged. So I've left more room in this reflections section.

Identify specific behaviors and how they have impacted your business. This is a simple exercise, but *don't underestimate* their importance. **Behaviors make or break your business** and leaders must be able to identify them, develop or stop them – theirs and others!

Start with this question => What are some profitable behaviors? Unprofitable?

Examples: Being cruel, abusive yelling – unprofitable, Making a positive coaching comment – profitable.

What behaviors are harmful to a team?....to customers?

Human Truth
Like decisions are building blocks
of your business, so are behaviors.

Expanded Discussion - Behaviors as a Business Asset

As mentioned, behaviors can make or break your business. This powerful truth demands attention and with that intentional strategies regarding how to leverage it.

One of the great advantages of behavior to business is that leaders can be intentional and strategic in creating them to serve an outcome.

For example if you want to lose weight – you *consistently* go to the gym...behavior => outcome. You create a behavior to get a desired result.

The catch to achieving the outcome in this case, however, is that the behavior needs to be *consistent*, repetitive long enough to get the result...*and for ultimate success,* the result needs to be reinforced and sustained.

In order to achieve this, the behavior therefore must become a **habit.** Repetition maps a neural pathway which creates a habit.

Habit defined: *A recurrent, often unconscious pattern of behavior that is acquired through frequent repetition. (American Heritage dictionary)*

In fact, the behavior becomes so consistent, one doesn't even have to consciously think about it anymore – it becomes an unconscious action. For example, have you ever driven home from work and wondered how you got there? Who drove you?...(besides a few angels?) You probably missed whole stretches of tress, had a few out of body experiences...and yet made it home safely. (I've even missed my exit a time or two).

Who or what drove you? Your unconscious – you're so expert at driving home you don't have to consciously thinking about it – in fact you can be thinking of other things while you're driving.

In human performance technology (htp), this is described as going from *conscious competence* - I have to intentionally think about it and work my will - to *unconscious competent* - I automatically do it without even thinking about it.

> The act of going from conscious behaving to unconscious behaving is commonly known as **conditioning**. It's also another description of a very popular word in leadership these days – transformation.
>
> What's really being described in this section is **changing** – going from one way of being or acting to another. Change can be temporary, transformation can make it permanent because it Is about change on a deeper level...it implies changing the very nature of something.

Here's the critical point, and human truth every leader should be acutely aware of: **humans are naturally habit forming beings**. We are naturally conditioned at every turn – without even realizing it.

Two definitions of conditioning for your consideration:

1
>predictable or consistent pattern of behavior or thought as a result of being subjected to certain circumstances or conditions.

2 >an acquired response that is under the control of (conditional on the occurrence of) a stimulus.

As a leader recognize…

> There is conditioning - <u>behaviors being shaped</u> – at your company **every day**. It's either helping or hurting what you want.

> *Every time* you interact with anyone, you are "conditioning" them as to what to expect from you. What you want, what you don't want. What you'll tolerate and won't. Their brain records your interactions for on-going reference.

> A company's culture serves as ongoing conditioning.

> A team culture provides ongoing conditioning.

> Interaction between employees are acts of conditioning.

This is all good if it serves the good.

Consider however, an unhealthy, dysfunctional manager…how does their behavior "condition" a team?...in what ways? What ripple effect does it create? How can that affect your business?

See, the natural act of conditioning can be helpful…*or not*. That's why you need to have a finely tuned sensibility about it.

This is the exact reason why there should be <u>zero tolerance</u> for unhealthy behavior from any employee…at any level.

Allowing its existence ***gives permission,*** (and might appear like approval) for counterproductive conditions and environments (commonly defined as "company culture") to **undermine the very things you are trying to achieve**. Do you want that?

Additionally consider…once someone, group or team is conditioned in a negative way, how much time it will take to undo what's been done…what's been recorded in their subconscious and which now *defines their experience* and attitudes about their current employment.

This is a very costly scenario that is difficult to reverse and will take time and money to do so!

It's also one in which talent will walk out the door (which just adds to the cost). Healthy, talented, confident people have a low tolerance for unhealthy people, atmospheres and leaders who are not actively and competently addressing issues.

The Dark Side of Conditioning
The Rise of the Bully & The Power Play

Please know that if you are not intentionally fostering a culture of good, it will create opportunities for bad behaviors to rein. One sinister behavior and personality in particular is the bully.

My colleague and strategic partner Suzi Benoitt, an expert regarding bullying in the workplace, shared the unique challenges.

Bullies and toxic employees use power in the workplace to their personal advantage. They control others through fear and manipulation. **They promote an informal power structure where they hold the power despite the fact that someone else has formal or "leadership" power.**

How this dynamic develops over time depends on the degree to which leadership is oblivious to the negative dynamics at play. (and the weakness of the culture In place.) These negative employees typically target either those they feel are vulnerable to manipulation or, those who threaten their power. They have a keen sense for what fear tactics will work best – otherwise known as "grooming."

An event takes place. Perhaps a new employee (target) who hasn't been fully "oriented" to the informal power structure approaches the bully and complains about something mean he or she has done to another employee. The bully's sensitive antenna is tuned to see this employee a s threatening their power.

Next, the bully retaliates by dressing them down in front of others, starting a rumor, or complaining to the target's supervisor about his/her performance. Once this gets back to the target, he/she will likely be horrified. You see, the new employee is vulnerable simply because negative feedback early on in a new job is exquisitely painful. Message received.

Bystanders who watch this happen understand the landscape. Over time, especially if no one dares confront the bully, good employees will leave and negative employees more comfortable in this negative environment will stay. Doing the math here, your culture degrades over time.

Reversing a long-standing negative atmosphere or culture takes significant time and effort and most likely an external resource with skill and experience in shifting culture.

It is actually easier to start the company having laid out the cultural road map but if the culture is already contaminated a sustained, concerted effort will be required.

Suzanne Benoit, LCSW, SPHR is an author, speaker, and consultant specializing in Human Resource strategy. Based in New England, she works with companies and HR professionals developing tools and solutions to a variety of employee relations challenges with a specialized expertise in workplace bullying and harassment.

Leadership Insight:
Personal power trumps positional power every time. In some teams, an individual wields more power than the positional manager. The leader is not empowered enough to use their personal nor positional power

A Few Additional Thoughts on Conditioning

> An employee survey is in essence gauging the "condition" of the current culture and the employees' "conditioned" experience (what they think and feel at that moment).

> Performance management – depending on how it's done – is really an attempt at conditioning desired behaviors and outcomes. That's why giving sporadic feedback is not very useful. Without regular, consistent feedback that's real-time and relevant, the opportunities for creating (conditioning) desired behaviors/performance – habits - are wasted.

> Purposely creating the conditions for a habit to from is an example of human performance technology (hpt). Part of the definition of technology is "a system or method".

> In fact, you ideally want to have strategic systems in place to create **productive, profitable habits**, which serve as the infrastructure of your operations.

Each individual and team currently has habits. Even a core, senior leadership team has habits. How are they aiding your desired outcomes… or not?

In summary, everything related to performance management, culture development, leadership & management, and operations utilizes the simple human truth that we are habit forming and are automatically conditioned. **A leader can allow it or intentionally leverage it.**

Leadership Reflection:
At this very moment identify some positive conditioning taking place in your organization. Is there any negative, counterproductive conditioning occurring? How about useful habits? …not so useful?

The Elephant & The Rope

As a man was passing the elephants, he suddenly stopped, confused by the fact that these huge creatures were being held by only a small rope tied to their front leg. No chains, no cages. It was obvious that the elephants could, at any time, break away from their bonds but for some reason, they did not.

He saw a trainer nearby and asked why these animals just stood there and made no attempt to get away. "Well," trainer said, "when they are very young and much smaller we use the same size rope to tie them and, at that age, it's enough to hold them. As they grow up, they are conditioned to believe they cannot break away. They believe the rope can still hold them, so they never try to break free."

The man was amazed. These animals could at any time break free from their bonds but because they believed they couldn't, they were stuck right where they were.

One item of note from this story – conditioning not only occurs with behaviors but thoughts and beliefs. Thinking can be habitual. Reactions due to triggers can be habitual. For example, *automatically* becoming angry or irritated at a thing or person over and over again (particularly when there is no present, relevant reason why) is an example of a conditioned response.

Human Truth
Negative conditioning sabotages talent development opportunities.

HABIT

"I am your constant companion; I am your greatest helper or your heaviest burden. I will push you onward or drag you down to failure. I'm completely at your command.

Half the things you do you might just as well turn over to me and I will be able to do them quickly and correctly. I am easily managed. You must merely be firm with me.

Show me exactly how you want something done and after a few lessons I will do it automatically. I am the servant of all great men and alas of all failures as well. Those who are great, I have made great. Those of you who are failures, I have made failures.

I am not a machine although I work with all the precision of a machine plus the intelligence of a man. You may run me for profit or run me for ruin. It makes no difference to me. Take me, train me, be firm with me and I'll put the world at your feet. Be easy with me and I will destroy you. Who am I? I am HABIT!"

Solidifying Your Leadership Effectiveness

Before moving on to the next section, I want to take a moment and pause. This section is such an important piece to bolstering your effectiveness. So, I want you to have an easy framework to use that fully integrates the information into your daily leadership and management.

This framework creates a coaching condition that <u>continually fosters improved results.</u> It's called "pac" – a slight twist on the word "pact". When you are wanting someone you lead to change, for most, *just telling them is not enough*. You'll need to "make a pac" with them.

Position an expectation. This is also positioning your *power* as the leader. This is important in case you meet resistance and the person really doesn't want to change what you desire. Then it becomes a test of wills or commonly known as a power play – whose "want " will win out. Knowing, understanding, and constructively working with power is essential in high-performing, effective leadership.

Question: Are you comfortable talking about and working with your positional power? You want to demonstrate *healthy positional power*.

Account – establish a way to demonstrate that you will be holding this person accountable. This is best done with daily or weekly follow ups (frequency is critical because you want to leverage natural habit formation). Frequency also provides the opportunity for clarity of expectations and continues to reinforce your positional power.

By the way, I think people are confused about what accountability really is. It's commonly used in business, but in some cases not actively used. See the definition below and notice the point about taking responsibility and "giving an account" for the activity around it. **Having to give account activates the a natural psychological pressure to change.**

Accountable definition:
1. Someone who is accountable is completely responsible for what they do and must be able to give a satisfactory reason for it:
2. Responsible for and having to explain your actions:
3. Responsible for what you do and able to give a satisfactory reason for it.
https://dictionary.cambridge.org/dictionary/english/accountable

Consistent – this person should know that you mean what you say – you mean what you expect. This message is conveyed by your consistency of account. If you're super busy, plug those brief meetings/conversations into your calendar – don't let them slip (or excuse them). They don't have to be formal or a big production – they just have to be consistent. The truth is if you don't deal with issues when needed, you'll have to take *more time* to deal with them (and perhaps larger consequences) later.

An essential element of your leadership effectiveness and healthy positional power *is being believed* – taken seriously. Consistency plays a vital role in that!

_ Notes _

Section 3 | Helping Leaders Develop Their Human Quotient

Humans Rock!

HQ Leadership™
Helping Leaders Develop Their Human Quotient
The Ultimate in Leadership Effectiveness

HQ Leadership defined: helping leaders be successfully attuned to and work with human behavior to improve business outcome.

< OVERVIEW >
Here's where our work has brought us to today.
We have developed *a literal* take on "human resources" -- your leaders and HR department should too!

Want to make managing your human resource real? Chart out the human elements that are impacted by leadership decisions and behaviors and one will see the *finely detailed components* of a company's "human resource" as well leadership effectiveness.

Leadership mind shift => These specific individual parts are *each* a valuable company resource *and* asset. Every day, leaders influence how they are manifested, so building awareness around this is critical!

With this chart as a framework, we teach leaders how "humans operate" and how to *positively* **activate, amplify, engage, impact, influence** these human elements through their day to day activities and leadership *for better outcomes in all areas* of the business.

We consider this list the **updated, modern leadership capabilities** that are *human-centered*. And from the information you've read so far, you can see why this is so essential. This type of discussion and information has not been a prominent part of leadership and management expectations in this past...and are barely on the radar today!

In addition to conditioning and neural leadership, this model will help leaders discover and identify their specific impact and are also practically able to determine if they are a meaningful business partner.

Quick Note: I mentioned earlier the conviction I have about fiscal stewardship. A meaningful business partner is one who is able to *profitably contribute* to a company's strategy, operational needs and bottom line. For example, if a manager due to unhealthy behavior, has difficulty with retention, a company is losing money. In this example, the manager is not demonstrating fiscal stewardship. If managers are causing financial loss, they are not meaningful business partners. So why do so many senior leaders allow it?

The Human Chart
Why is this chart so important? As a reminder, *every behavior caused or influenced is either serving business outcomes or not,* utilizing the compensation investment of each employee or not.

Also with this chart, we can *practically* bring to life commonly used leadership terms like **empower, inspire and engage** – showing exactly where and how they occur. We've discovered most don't really know what those words mean or how they are *tangibly demonstrated*.

This chart along with the other information contained in this book is the ultimate in 21st century insights regarding how to maximize human performance and the leader-follow dynamic. Every element of this chart is regularly influenced in a positive or negative way by a company's **environment, culture and leadership**.

If there are any employee performance problems, it will most likely come from and can be positively addressed from this chart.

So this is also a great tool to use when diagnosing operational or organizational issues and determining whether to coach up or coach out.

Leadership Insight
You cannot change what you do not know and cannot not see.

It All Happens Between the Lines
The Human Quotient in Detail

To describe good leadership and management, we use a variety of words to describe desired qualities and actions – for example, "inspirational". Yet many don't know what these qualities really mean and how to *practically* implement or demonstrate them.

Since we work with the essence of the human experience, we've been able to practically identify how to express these qualities and their results.

We've even gone one step further. We can explain the financial impact, which we do in our briefing book *Show Me the Money, and which we'll give an introduction to in Section 4.*

In order to **clearly show and explain the impact of leadership and management actions on the human experience**, we created a "human" chart. Here leaders can learn how to specifically identify their impact, where the impact is being made and if they are helping or hurting their own cause.

This chart is another example of how we use and explain the phrase "human resource" in the most literal sense. It's much more than just a department – *it is a composite of all aspects of what makes us human and how those aspects are applied to business operations every day.*

The Human Experience
Beyond thinking, feeling and behaving, we can use the well-known areas of mind, body, spirit to define the human experience. I've broken down these areas further, focusing specifically on mind and spirit as they relate to activity in business.

We give a brief description of each, though some are commonly understood. A few will have a bit more information. What's important to glean from this section is whatever happens in your business *is experienced* through any one of these "human elements", which again we term *the human quotient* in business.

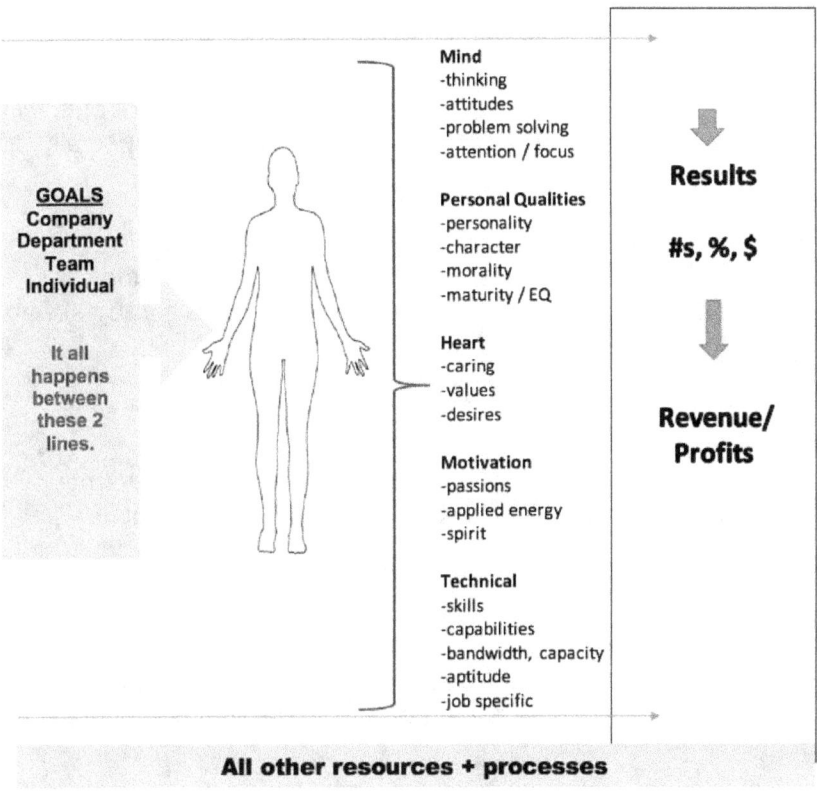

Stop and Consider
- ✓ **Every single thing** on this chart *is* a business resource.
- ✓ Human qualities – the composite of a human being - are business critical assets.
- ✓ A company cannot run without any of the above.
- ✓ **Every** employee problem can be tied to at least one element on this chart.

Critical business leadership & management question:
How are you, your leaders and managers working with the elements of this chart?

< The Human Quotient: Definitions >

Mind
Think – have a conscious mind, to some extent of reasoning, remembering experiences, combining values and beliefs, that can lead to conclusions, judgments, making decisions, etc.

Attitude - manner, disposition, feeling, position, mind-set etc., with regard to a person or thing; tendency or orientation, especially of the mind:

Problem solving - the process of working through details of a problem to reach a solution. Problem solving may include mathematical or systematic operations and can be a gauge of an individual's critical thinking skills.

Focus - a central point, as of attraction, attention, or activity

Attention - a state of consciousness characterized by such concentration; a capacity to maintain selective or sustained concentration: observant care; consideration:

Personality / Qualities
Personality - the organized pattern of behavioral characteristics of the individual: the visible aspect of one's character as it impacts others:

Note: Personality creates preferences; for example how someone likes to work, what they value, how they assess and respond to the world around them, workstyle.

Character - the aggregate of features and traits that form the individual nature of some person or thing: moral or ethical quality

Morality - conformity to the rules of right conduct; moral or virtuous conduct.

Maturity - developed in body, mind, emotion, as a person:. Capable of being responsible ("response – able") as necessary to any particular context; capable of functioning in a socially appropriate way. Here I think we are all on a journey. Age is not necessarily a reflection of maturity. Rarely is someone wholly mature in every context all the time.

Emotional /Social Intelligence - The ability to identify, assess and influence one's own feelings and those of others and manage and respond appropriately.

Note: The element of maturity is the #1 issue related to unproductive or dysfunctional employee performance.

Heart
Heart - the center of the total personality, especially with reference to intuition, feeling, or emotion

Caring – to feel concern about; to wish, desire, like

Values - to consider with respect to worth, excellence, usefulness, or importance: what matters most

Desires - to wish or long for; crave; want; to express a wish to obtain; ask for; request: / seat of passion

Motivation
Motivations - Internal and external factors that *stimulate* desire and *energy* in people to be continually interested and committed to a job, role or subject, or to make an effort to attain a goal.

Motivation results from the interaction of both conscious and unconscious factors such as…

(1) intensity of desire or need
(2) incentive or reward value of the goal, and
(3) expectations of the individual and of his or her peers.

These factors **are the reasons** one has for behaving a certain way…give reason = *motive*

Morale – group motivation, energy, spirit

Human Truth
Motivation is a human resource.

Passion(s) - any powerful or compelling emotion or feeling, as love or hate: strong amorous feeling or desire; love; ardor.

Energy - the capacity for vigorous activity; available power

Spirit - the soul or heart as the seat of feelings or sentiments, or as prompting to action: the principle of conscious life; the vital principle in humans, animating the body or mediating between body and soul; the core essence of someone; life force.

I mentioned earlier we understand the essence of the human experience, can determine how commonly used words in leadership are practically demonstrated. Here, **inspire** would apply. To inspire is to *activate the life force* of someone that then motivates them to action. (*feel alive, give energy to*)

Examples: How do you feel when you come out of motivational speech or event; after a great sermon at church, a major achievement at a sporting event: hearing someone's personal story of overcoming adversity…. There are many sources of inspiration, so it doesn't have to be in "big" things, even the smallest, thoughtful acts can "inspire" – activate someone's spirit!

Another example; encourage – to give, instill courage. Courage is motivating…it activates the spirit. One of my favorite quotes in leadership: "Give someone your courage, until they can gain their own."

Technical
Skills – exceptional ability: competent excellence in performance; expertness

Capabilities – having power and ability

Bandwidth - mental capacity; intelligence: a person's capacity to handle or think about more than one thing at the same time:

Capacity - the ability to receive or contain:
power of receiving impressions, knowledge, etc.; mental ability: the maximum amount or number that can be received or contained

Aptitude - capability; ability; innate or acquired capacity for something; talent: readiness or quickness in learning; intelligence.

Job specific – activities related to job description, job functions, job specific knowledge.

Leadership Side Bar | Are You "Dissin'" Your Employees?

It happens a lot you know. Dissin' is a great slang word to describe the negative experience of an employee in a variety of ways and which can be easily identified from our human chart.

Consider the following…
- Disrespect
- Dis**heart**en
- Di**spirit**
- Disown
- Disable
- Disem**power** *(motivation)*
- Discount
- Discourage
- Dishonor

And when you "diss" them, here's what can happen:

- Teams can become disjointed
- Relationships can become disconnected
- Individuals become disinterested
- Disengaged
- Distracted
- Distrusted
- Disturbed
- Disaffected
- Disenchanted
- Disappointed
- Disgusted
- Disloyal

And these are just a few – add your own and mark up the human chart accordingly. Go back and review the definitions.

An Important & Expanded Discussion
Use of the word "skills"

This word is grossly misused in the training and development industry. We must make a clear distinction between skills & capabilities. The following is an edited excerpt from our video learning brief *The Fundamentals of Adult Learning:*

"We're going to look at the three most commonly misused terms in the training industry. I really want you to be keenly aware and sensitive to these as you move forward. Here's the three that we typically use: **learning, training, and skill.**

For example, if you were to see a brochure from a seminar company and they say, "when you leave this seminar, you will learn these skills or you will have these skills." That is completely not true because a skill is something you **know how to do well**, so talking *about* a skill or learning about a skill…does not a skill make.

When we're making decisions about employee training, we've got to be very clear about what we expect. So when we're talking about learning, what we're really talking about is knowledge acquisition.

Knowledge acquisition is a prelude to developing a skill, or sometimes we just need to expand our knowledge base so we have the needed resource by which to make different decisions or improve job performance - for example customer service. You have to know the product to know how to apply good customer service related to the product. You have to have an appropriate knowledge base. **Knowledge acquisition is learning, but is not necessarily "training".**

Next developing. There is a distinction between knowing something and doing something. *Learning something is not the same as developing a behavior,* developing a habit or achieving a behavior change.

Unfortunately, we interchange the word training with learning. So we would say, "Hey, I just trained someone." What we really are saying is, "We just increased their knowledge."

Training in the truest sense is when you develop new behaviors or skills. For example, if you go to the gym you don't sit in front of a screen and look at a PowerPoint. You actually take action, you have a coach, you do reps, there's physical involvement because *it's in the repetition* that the behavior change occurs, develops the muscles, et cetera. (Remember our section on conditioning).

> We grossly misuse and interchange learning and training when what we really mean is learning or want is developing behavior change.

And then finally, we *really* misuse the word skill. Skill is something that we know how to do well. We use skill when what we really mean is capable. There are people who are **capable** *(key word here)* of doing things that may not yet be skilled.

Here's a great example. I am quite capable of managing a conversation that contains conflict. I don't like conflict, but I'm capable of doing it. Am I highly skilled at it? I'm trying to get there. *But just because I'm capable of doing it doesn't mean I'm skilled at it.* That is a very important distinction.

So when we use the word skill what we typically mean is they are **capable of doing it to an acceptable degree**.

It doesn't mean, "Man, that person is just really, really good at that thing." That's *maximum competency* and very few people are really skilled in the soft skills – for example, managing conflict, negotiating or coaching an employee.

We could ask, "How many people do you know, for example are like the Michael Jordan of coaching?" Very few. Now they may be very capable of coaching and are capable to a certain level or degree – even an acceptable or useful degree, but they may not be the Michael Jordan of coaching.

This is the distinction we need to make when we're using these terms.

In summary, we want to make sure that we understand the distinction between learning and developing, and between being capable and skilled.

Again, just to reiterate, a lot of times when we're talking about employee training, what we're talking about is *employee learning*. True training takes longer. It takes more investment. It takes time because there's behavior change involved.

A lot of money is wasted in the training and development industry due to not making these distinctions.

Summary
As a leader or manager, in effectively managing your human resource - in its more literal sense – all of the vocabulary above must be clearly understood and reflected in how you lead and manage your teams, including your HR department.

> I can trace *all* mismanagement to the lack of understanding and awareness of these human elements and how they relate to leading, building and managing a business.

Human Truths
Managing is conditioning.
A habit is a form of technology
known as human performance technology or HPT.

| Leadership Side Bar |

Your Own Human Resource
How's Your Bandwidth & Capacity?

I happen to part of a very entrepreneurial family. Of the 8 adults in our immediate family (kids & spouses) we own and run 5 businesses in different parts of the country! Between my husband and I, there is regular discussions about bandwidth (he started one and bought into another as a partner).

We can tell when bandwidth is being stretched because we both feel stressed. Now that's not necessary bad, it is, however, something to be aware of and monitor. Not doing so can lead to burnout!

When you start saying, "I don't know how much more of this I can take…"… it's time to start having conversations with appropriate help to monitor and sort through what's happening.

It could also be a reason why a newly promoted manager or leader is not functioning well or someone in a new role struggles. Bandwidth and capacity definitely relate to being overwhelmed, the capacity to successfully execute new responsibilities.

Everyone is due an adjustment period, however, this is also something that needs to be supported and monitored. If performance continues to decline, it may get to a point of no return – damaging the self-esteem, self-confidence of the manager or employee, along with other unfortunate business consequences.

This is one reason we offer Executive Support by serving as a sounding boarding, helping sort through decision-making, being a confidant and trusted advisor.

Leadership Reflection:
Take some time to really think about these two human elements. How do they related to you?...members of your team?

Power & Responsibility
The Ultimate Leadership Challenge of the Human Quotient

An element of the human quotient no one wants to acknowledge or talk about is suffering. You'd be hard pressed to find a leader eager to entertain the possibility that the daily variety of actions and decisions executed actually cause their employees to suffer.

No one really wants to accept that they cause suffering.

Yet, that's the kind of power leaders possess and why improving their 'human quotient' is so critical.

That's also the reason why emotionally immature leaders with power are destructive to an organization. They cause self-serving suffering to those they lead (and some really unhealthy folks actually get off on it).

Suffering is defined as pain, distress; forced to endure; emotionally, mentally, spiritually or physically.

Now suffering for sure is inevitable, like grief and can be useful for building character – successfully managing suffering is a life skill.

However, without the awareness and *care* regarding the human experience of suffering – many leaders will make "care-less" decisions with blinders.

This is what some call "heart-less". (You can see how these relate to the human chart). The *ability* and *willingness* to make decisions when attuned to suffering is called **empathy.**

When a leader with high EQ (emotional intelligence quotient) & HQ (human quotient) has to make tough decisions, how much suffering is weighted and influences plans. There is an authentic desire to mitigate it as much as possible in light of what needs to be done.

I can safely say that almost all complaints about a company's leadership, management or customer service is related to the their inability to connect with and meaningfully acknowledge suffering – even in the smallest measure.

Human Truth: Complaining is a result of suffering - legitimate or not.
Even HR Professionals Can Improve their HQ!

Compassionately working with suffering is an exceptional leadership quality.

Following Rules with Heart
Steven Johnson, MBA, PHR, SHRM-CP | Author, *The Book on FMLA*

I fell into managing FMLA for my employer. And when I did, all I had heard about FMLA was how much it is abused by employees. My mindset upon taking it over was we just have to put up with it. To be sure, we have to comply with the law.

As I got into my new responsibility, I did not find a mountain of abuse. Most of our employees were using FMLA for legitimate reasons - their own or their eligible family member's serious health condition.

What I did find was some managers had not been given the tools to manage employees who were using FMLA. My approval process changed to improve the information provided to managers.

Managers may have previously been informed with something similar to, "Your employee is approved for FMLA from this date to that date." If the time between those dates was a few weeks, I assume the employee was off work consecutively. If the dates were twelve months apart, then time off was probably taken intermittently. My new approvals grew to several paragraphs.

Not only did the manager know the beginning and ending dates and consecutive or intermittent use, they were informed about whether an employee is using FMLA for appointments or those dreaded episodic flare-ups. I realized everything on that page of the employee medical certification is related to attendance. Perfect information that the manager needs to know, separated from medical information the manager isn't to know.

The first time a manager told me how helpful it was to know that her employee could have three flare-ups in a month and be off work for a day each episode, I felt like I found my calling. Beyond that, our FMLA approval for an employee had always been sent to the employee's manager with the employee receiving a copy of that communication. Improving the approval process meant communicating with the employee directly, while the manager receives the copy.

Over time, I continued to research FMLA, even developing a conference presentation to help my fellow Human Resources professionals.

Steven's HQ Moment

Then one day, my telephone rang. A manager who had been on my FMLA journey with me, told me she has an employee in need of FMLA for her son. The employee said she had no idea how FMLA could help her. I started to respond with my usual, "FMLA is to take off work to care for him." I could tell she was in distress over not being able to do anything to help her son. I took a deep breath and said softly, "I'm sorry you're going through this. I'll help in any way I can."

Neither of us said anything for a moment, then I added that FMLA is also so she can take time for herself. I needed some details in order to guide her correctly. I had to ask questions that I already knew the answer to. I had to hear the response and not make assumptions. But that doesn't mean I have to act without compassion.

"I need to ask you some questions. Is what you're going through bad enough that it could affect how you do your job?" Yes. "Are there days that you can't come to work because of this?" Yes again. "Can a doctor confirm this?" A third yes.

A sense of relief came over me. I knew there's no turning back. *I could help an employee and make sure we do things right* at the same time. I told her that I needed documentation to make it official, but that she would qualify for leave and it wouldn't be counted against her.

I often wondered if she knew how much that meant to me or impacted me. Maybe someday I'll tell her she has a special place in my heart.

Steven Johnson, MBA, PHR, SHRM-CP, is author of *The Book on FMLA*. He is a favorite at SHRM events sharing his expertise on the nuances of successfully administering FMLA. You can connect with him at his website and to find the link to Amazon to obtain his book. He is currently Human

Resources Coordinator at Health & Hospital Corporation of Marion County, Indiana | www.stevencolejohnson.com

The Human Quotient – The Role of Human Energy
Can You Read Human Behavior like the Beach Boys?

Have you ever been around a person for a bit or walked into a room and said, "Boy I just feel some bad vibes."

Or, you spend time with someone and walk away thinking, "I feel so good when I'm around them." They have such a good vibe.

The word "vibe" has been around for quite some time. Harken back to the early sixties and you can still hear echoes of the Beach Boys' song..."I'm picking up good vibrations". The Beach Boys' read regarding human interaction is really quite scientific (...of course I don't know if they *really* knew that) and is also what we need in leadership today!

Vibe is a shorten representation of the word vibration.

And though you may not see them, you can feel them -- vibrations do exist. If you've never used it or heard of it, here is how it is defined in the urban dictionary:

> *Noun: A distinctive emotional atmosphere; sensed intuitively; feeling, atmosphere, aura*

Though vibe seems to be derived from and seen as the language of the 60's era, little did we know back then how scientific that word was and how a lot of social lingo or slang we use, even today, is grounded in that science..."feelin' me?" *(emotional intelligence).*

Though you may not use vibe as a part of your everyday lingo, it is inescapably built into our human existence and impacts every element of who we are and what we do.

> *By the way, leaders have a vibe. A company brand has a vibe.*

Vibe represents energy and we experience the qualities of that energy whenever we interact.
There is a universal energy that connects us all and we experience it whether we're aware of it or not. We are interconnected to a variety of energy elements within the universe.

So, for starters, there is an individual vibe - the metaphysical term could be considered an individual's spirit or essence of who they are. It is the source that dictates how we interact with others and also contributes to the collective vibe of a group.

"...there is a fortuitous connection between the physiology of consciousness, the function of the nervous system and the physics of the universe." *David Hawkins, Power vs. Force*

Side note: another word familiar to many to describe vibe is *chemistry*.

Here's the cool thing, published science surrounding the idea of "vibe" or chemistry has finally become more mainstream and intersected with what we've been intuiting and experiencing as humans for quite some time.

Here's two examples:
> The discovery of mirror neurons in the brain that detect smiles and laughter and causes a similar response. (You can read more about this in the Harvard Business Review article <u>Social Intelligence and the Biology of Leadership</u>).

> The energy level of certain human qualities calibrated though muscle testing in the work done by <u>David Hawkins, Power vs. Force</u>.

In essence, we have and experience unseen connections with one another that greatly influences every aspect of ourselves and can be used to assess how teams work, how leaders impact followers and ultimately a company's results.

So, let's think about leadership for a moment. We can safely say, and it has been proven scientifically, that a leader's vibe affects their followers in very distinct ways. It means that how a leader relates can reach and impact positively or negatively the *core essence* or spirt of a person they lead, *i.e.* their vibe.

The quality and intensity of their vibe can influence a certain level of motivation and how that person will act or respond in their surroundings. I believe this is where *personality conflicts* can arise or "not clicking" with someone for no logical reason.

Think about this for a moment.
It's quite powerful!
It also holds good news and potentially bad.

Here's the point, though studies have been conducted and new science revealed, I've seen this through-out my entire work life. I bet you have too!

Honestly, we don't need a plethora of studies and science to tell us what we see and experience everyday regarding a boss, leader, or manager's impact on team members (or team members on each other).

However, for those who seem to resist these truths, they (the studies and science) do come in handy to share.

So, when helping leaders become more effective, helping business owners build company cultures that can consistently thrive, their ability to know, see and understand how *they affect <u>the very essence</u> of those they lead is critical.* We call that their Human Quotient *(tm)*.

Leaders need to expand beyond their EQ to HQ.

Why? Because *ultimately,* <u>this *is* **THE** Source</u> of an employee's motivation to participate and perform or be engaged.

There essence is where it all begins (refer back to human chart). **The source becomes <u>the force</u>** for a fountain of motivation. *This is the true essence of a company's "human resource".*

So we can firmly say, **an employee's spirit, or essence is the ultimate human resource, from which everything else flows.** The more a company connects to this, the more engaged and loyal an employee will be. They will give *willing* and want to stay.

> *Very important point* > how a leader touches, reaches, impacts this will influence everything else regarding how that employee behaves and contributes.
>
> An employee's essence or spirit is expressed through, gives life to, their heart, mind and physical actions. How they are treated can deeply impact that. **_It is the lifeblood of their humanity._**

And so, consider this, if an employee is treated "inhumanely", it could diminish the very essence of who they are and what they have and are willing to give...unless they are strong enough and aware enough to respond in strength, to victoriously manage the adverse impact of those actions.

To be able to do this takes strong character and personal maturity. Many employees can manage even the subtlest of inhumane treatment...though it takes a rare person to do so for an extended period of time. That's why if someone has a bully boss and there is little hope of change, I advise them to leave that boss, team or company.

Equally, for as many employees that can adequately handle a broad range of inhumane behavior, please know **there are *many more* who can't**.

Disregarding someone's spirit - treating someone inhumanely from a tiny act to significant is a talent killer!.. and turn an advocate into an advisory.

If this is not acknowledged and truly taken to heart in leadership and HR, you can throw any discussion about employee engagement out the window.

It's like asking a car to travel without gas. Many leaders and managers relate in a way that adds zero gas and yet expects that car to keep on driving and in fact act or perform like a Ferrari!

Here's my observation:
__Most leaders expect, mostly on a subconscious level, their employees, in the midst of inhumane treatment, to be superhuman.__

Effective leadership is knowing what you're working with to get the best results. Yet few leaders *really* know how to work with the core elements of their "human resource" and therefore allow a broad range of inhumane treatment with *little regard or awareness of its impact.*

A lot of the challenges in leading could and should be addressed in this way. It would certainly diminish many "employee problems", staring with a leadership value and commitment to dignity:

Defined as:
Dignity is the <u>right</u> of a person to be valued and respected for their own sake, and to be treated ethically.
(source-Wikipedia)

It's time we as a leadership and business owner community learned and applied these human truths. We are becoming a more *conscious* society regarding how folks are treated in the workplace, particularly due to the surge in sexual harassment awareness.

The recent steady flow of revelations are also nurturing more social *conscience* about how we treat others in general, along with the continual advocation for diversity and inclusion.

Simply put... are we aware and do we care? (Great example of this, at the time of this writing, <u>the Women's Gymnastics Team</u> and <u>Michigan State Athletics</u>.)

Leaders Can Be Either Drains or Fountains

"They can either nourish you and help you grow as a person or they can stunt your growth and make you wilt and die." - Plato

When working with leaders and business owners to help them build positive, empowered work cultures to produce operations that flourish...this is what we look at and learn about.

We go to the essence of what it means to be human first, before we attach a leadership title and teach them exactly, and *practically* how to positively and constructively work with all aspects of the human element.

We help then connect being human to business building.

They have been blown away by the insights to their leadership challenges they've obtained when understanding the role the human experience plays in operational performance and outcomes.

> How is your vibe as a leader (your vibe reflects and communicates who you really are...whether you're aware or not)?

> How would others describe your vibe when they experience you?

> What does your vibe activate in others? Is it a fountain or a drain?

> Does it activate positive behaviors or negative, constructive or destructive, productive or counterproductive?

> Does your leadership positively enliven and even amplify the heart, mind and spirit of each of your employees?

> How is the vibe of your team?

> Do you have any toxic vibes on your team? (This is very destructive, take it seriously!)

> How is the spirit of your team? These concepts give new meaning to the phrase "team spirit" and "team chemistry".

> Does your leadership and team have a vibe that generates high energy qualities? (High energy qualities generate motivation, creativity, synergy, constructive collaboration, work satisfaction connection, voluntary participation and contribution...to name a few)

Please know, the answers to these questions have a direct impact on your P/L. Believe me!

The Human Quotient: Meet My Needs & I'll Meet Yours

"if you care about me, I'll care about what you want me to care about."

I have been amazed at an interesting finding in working with clients and studying the success of companies in general.

Here's the discovery – the more a company meets the core human/personal needs of employee the more loyal they are and the more they willingly contribute.

I've worked with companies in which I've discussed this as a leadership and management practice beginning at a 1 to 1 level between a manger and employee, all the way to the senior leadership strategy for business management and culture development.

Maslow's Hierarchy of Need
If you're not familiar with the concept of Maslow's Hierarchy of Needs, here's a quick refresher:

Maslow's hierarchy of needs is a motivational theory in psychology comprising a five-tier model of human needs, often depicted as hierarchical levels within a pyramid.

Needs lower down in the hierarchy must be satisfied before individuals can attend to needs higher up. From the bottom of the hierarchy upwards, the needs are: physiological, safety, love and belonging, esteem and self-actualization.

Note the chart to follow…

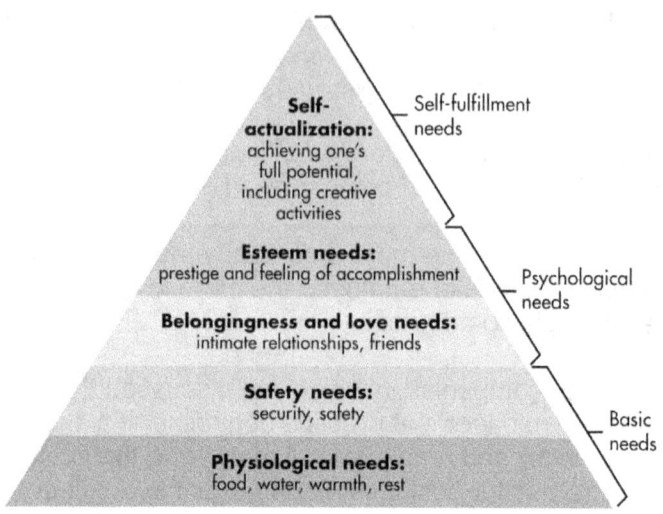

You can use this link for more information – it's the source for the information above: https://simplypsychology.org/maslow.html

Now let's keep in mind Maslow's hierarchy and make the connection to the employee experience and participation. The following chart does so in an interesting way. It's also a useful chart to plan human resource and talent management strategies for development and retention.

Notes:

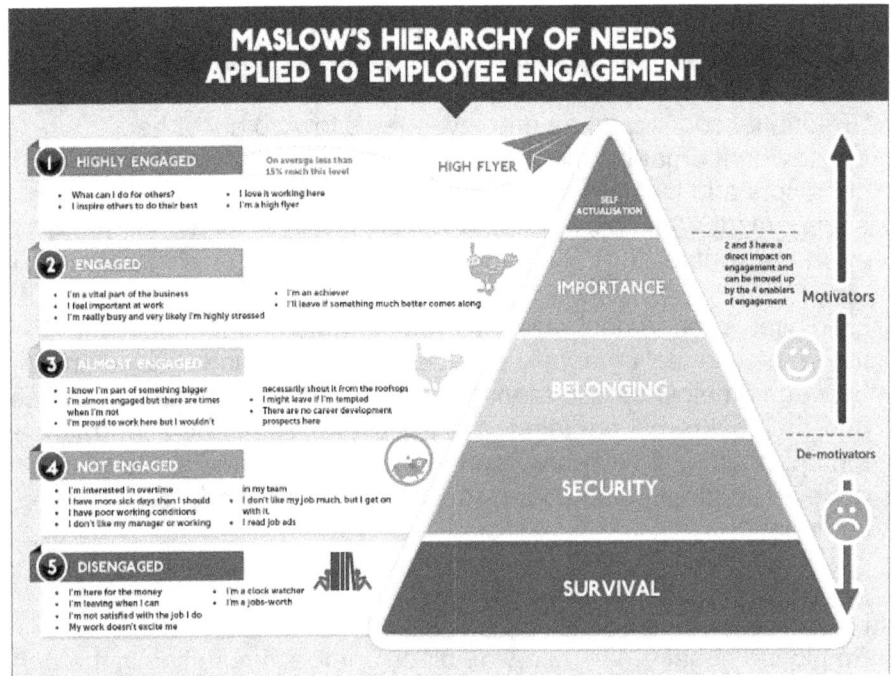

Source link: http://www.hrzone.com/community-voice/blogs/steve-smith-0/how-maslows-hierarchy-of-needs-influences-employee-engagement

In reviewing this chart, it's easy to see where the relationship with a manager fits as well as a company's culture and management practices all influencers related to popular term "employee engagement.

An Expanded Discussion - Employee Engagement

I have to confess, I am not a big fan of this phrase. To me it is another example of contrived lingo by my industry (human resource, talent management) and complicates how we see the human experience in business. Someone came up with it, folks caught on to it ..now it's a big deal, though there is still not one standard definition.
Never the less, a whole industry of consultants and assessments have cropped up around it.

So what is it and how can we connect it to the human quotient.

First, let's look at a fairly comprehensive definition:

This is from the Business Dictionary and one of the best I've found. I've italicized key words that we want to give special attention to:

"*Emotional connection* an employee *feels* toward his or her employment organization, which tends to influence his or her behaviors and level of effort in work related activities. The more engagement an employee has with his or her company, the more effort they put forth.

Employee engagement also involves the nature of the job itself - if the employee feels mentally stimulated; the trust and communication between employees and management; ability of an employee to see how their own work contributes to the overall company performance; the opportunity of growth within the organization; and the level of pride an employee has about working or being associated with the company."
http://www.businessdictionary.com/definition/employee-engagement.html

I also like this one:
Employee engagement is a workplace approach resulting in the right conditions for all members of an organization to give of their best each day, committed to their organization's goals and values, motivated to contribute to organizational success, with an enhanced sense of their own well-being.
https://engageforsuccess.org/what-is-employee-engagement

Take a moment to read through the definitions in light of the 3 charts we've presented. You'll notice a lot of the definition is centered around the "feeling" element of the human experience and some behaviors and the most is about **perception.**

You may want to go back to the feeling, thinking section of the book. We've learned feelings develop through our thinking (and triggers), our shaped experience and how we describe it to ourselves – the story or interpretation we give it.

In fact the human quotient is embedded in every definition of employee engagement you'll read. Why (and I can confidently say this without reading every one) because by its very nature engagement and it's definition is about the human experience at a particular place of employment and that is the essence of the human quotient.

We could say that any measurement taken from an engagement survey, an opinion survey or an employee survey of any kind is an attempt to measure the human quotient.

[A Thought on Measuring: Feelings vary day to day and are rarely consistent in volume or intensity. So how can they be appropriately measured? For an attempt to measure, we can use a continuum to identify patterns and levels over a period of time. Just like in pain management, they don't ask are you feeling pain or not, they use a scale…identifying the pain intensity on a scale of 1-10. This is why in the next section when we discuss KPIs, we recommend daily or weekly monitoring of a team's pulse, which is included in our 5 Step Predictive Leadership & Business Management System.]

We can also say that addressing employee engagement is also about managing employee perception. It's working with the company and leadership's internal brand.

What's great about this briefing is that every piece of information, if taken to heart and applied, can positively and directly affect your employees' engagement. And, it's not rocket science…just a bit of people science applied in practical ways.

For example, just cultivating a more positive team atmosphere affects engagement. Nurturing more authentic, respectful relationships strengthens connections and enhances perceptions resulting in increased engagement.

Leadership Tip:
Please do not waste money on employee engagement surveys, if you are not and have no intention of investing in management development. For years, it's been said that the number one reason people leaves jobs Is due to their bosses.

The most significant impact to employee engagement, therefore, is a manager's ability to foster positive, respectful, relationships and lead competently.

One Final Note
I do believe too much focus on 'engagement' can become a bit of navel gazing and can serve as a distraction from the most important business issue - achieving desired results.

Here's an interesting question: If you're getting the business outcomes you want, does the "level" of engagement matter...particularly in light of the definitions presented?

| EXAMPLES |

I love LinkedIn. I have the great opportunity to be a learning partner as an subject matter expert, course author. I get the opportunity to visit one of their campuses to produce and film my courses. Every time I'm there, I feel welcomed and cared for.

Their staff is talented, personable, courteous, helpful and supportive. And yes, at this is campus is a foosball table, a ping pong table, pictures on walls of employee art work, pictures of their kids, free food for breakfast and lunch, plus drinks and snacks oh plenty!

On days we're filming we don't have to leave campus, but saunter over to the "cafeteria"...eat, visit and relax. The atmosphere is comfortable and professionally casual. I love watching people interact as I walk around the campus and eat in the cafeteria. You can tell people really enjoy being together.

Where you find humans, you will always find problems, so I'm not suggesting perfection. In general, as I've talked to the folks I've worked with, there is a genuine sense of enjoyment in working with and being part of the LinkedIn family.

From what I know of the LinkedIn culture and practices, as with other tech companies, (and those who've made the list of Best Places to Work) - https://www.glassdoor.com/Award/Best-Places-to-Work-LST_KQ0,19.htm every aspect of Maslow's chart is met in substantial ways.

No wonder they have no problem recruiting. Google for example gets thousands of resumes a year! Here's an article that suggests the reasons why.

Cracking Into Google: 15 Reasons Why More Than 2 Million People Apply Each Year :
https://www.forbes.com/sites/stanphelps/2014/08/05/cracking-into-google-the-15-reasons-why-over-2-million-people-apply-each-year/#392939b82038

This also reminds me of a recent event a friend helped to coordinate for her company. Pictures were shared on a LinkedIn post. The event pictures attracted many comments reflecting how they loved working for the company and how much they appreciated the opportunity for personal and professional growth.

Reflect for a moment on the examples above. What part of the "human chart" do these examples hit?

Though you may not have the resources to do exactly what Google or LinkedIn does, the question is *what can you do* to ensure needs at all levels of Maslow's chart are met?

Decision Insight

When thinking about spending money on employees in any way, think of it as *an intentional investment*.

You are literally investing in their mind, thinking, mindset, attitude, heart, desire, passions, motivation, energy, capacity, technical knowledge, maturity and internal leadership/company brand (how employees see your leadership)...etc.

For example: Posta Plus, a client that specializes in courier and logistics services, had a huge ice cream day in three different countries (UAE, Kuwait, and Bahrain) because it was super-hot.. Look at all three charts, where was the investment?

For sure – physical need, the attitudes of the employees and how they feel about the company which could nurture loyalty, individual motivation, group motivation, collective attitude & motivation = morale.

What could be **the ripple effect**? ...more motivation? => tell friends at the next gathering => talented friend says, "Man, that's a place I'd like to work. Can you refer me?"=>You interview and see this is a person you'd like to hire.=> He goes on to do great work.

All that...from buying some ice cream!

Many leaders suffer from "fos", fear of spending. I have seen one of the main reasons is they don't know how to identify, measure, or quantitate their return.

Reminder: Since your human resource is your #1 business resource...then that is what you're investing in. Also many leaders take for granted "the ripple effect" both positive and negative!

Leadership Reflection: Take my story and match it to both the human chart and Maslow's chart. Record your thoughts –think about your business. How are you currently addressing both charts? How much, which ones and to what degree? Are there any opportunities for improvement?

Rules of Engagement
A Story of Dignity, Respect, Compassion, & Heart

I've had the opportunity to marry into an amazing family. Our immediate family has 4 business owners and all of the adult children are leaders in their respective fields – one of which is in the military.

Yes…leadership and the human quotient even apply to the military. As you read this story, keep in mind the human chart…

Onboard my first ship, a destroyer out of Mayport, Florida, we were due to leave for a month and a half exercise. This was not a 'real world' operation, rather training in preparation for an upcoming deployment to the Mediterranean. One of the sailors in my division was an expecting father, but the mother was not due to have the baby until after our return.

Several weeks into the exercise, the sailor got news that both the mother and baby were experiencing severe complications. This of course weighed heavily on his mind, but we were due to pull into port in Nassau, The Bahamas later in the week. The request went up the chain of command to allow him to go on leave to be with them. The sailor was not needed as he was still training and not even a backup for any of our primary roles.

The request was ultimately denied despite several rather vehement intercessions on his behalf at each level up the chain of command. That sailor ended up considering disobeying orders and going to the airport in Nassau to book himself a flight home. Had he taken this option, he could have been demoted, fined, or even kicked out of the military.

The rest of the exercise, this Sailor was distracted to the point of being unsafe. There are countless ways to get seriously injured onboard a warship at sea, even if your head is in the game. If he was not on watch he could be found leaning on the weather lines, looking towards the horizon with a blank stare. In his mind he was a thousand miles away, flipping from worst case scenario to the next, wondering if he would be able to live with himself if this took a tragic turn.

This demoralized not only the sailor, but everyone on that ship. The leadership had sent a clear message that they did not see people, but instead saw only boxes to be checked and seats that needed to be filled. While at this command, I could not get off watch or leave the ship soon enough. Every time I returned from leave, I felt my heart sink.

Years later, while in the middle of a transfer between duty-stations, my wife was diagnosed with leukemia. Leadership at both my previous and new commands were beyond supportive. I could not have gone into work if I tried. Instead, I was told to spend my time with her in the hospital and to call in each morning and each day I was asked if there was anything that we needed. Other folks at work even went a step further, delivering food, and offering support.

When it came time to move into our new home, the Chief Master at Arms, who I had been talking to each day, asked me when and where he was sending a 6-person working party to help get the house ready, cleaned up, and moved in. I had insisted that I did not need or want the help, but I was quickly reminded that this was not a request.

My wife ultimately finished her third round of chemotherapy shortly afterwards and was later given the news that she was in full remission. Words cannot express the sense of overwhelming relief and joy experienced in that moment.

When I did go back to work, I did not have the constant worry eating away at me each day distracting me from the task at hand. Beyond that, my command had treated me like a human-being, even like family. This gave me 'buy-in' each day I came to work. I had a reason beyond personal motivation to ensure that my leadership and my command succeeded. They had shown me that I was important; not just what I could do for them, but that I mattered. When someone needed to stay late to provide training, or someone was needed for a short-notice deployment to Iraq, I was the first to volunteer.

Some people show up to work and meet minimum standards, only trying to avoid negative consequences. Others take a vested interest in the success of their team. The difference goes beyond what is offered in a compensation package, or someone's personal motivation, it is often directly tied to whether that person was treated compassionately, as a human being with dignity, or as just another cog in the machine. - *Chief Petty Officer David Schwarzkopf (Thank you for your service David!)*

[In each of the examples spread through-out this book, you could go through the charts and note the impact where and to what degree. Doing so, helps you continue to build awareness.]

Before you move on, I recommend you take a moment to record some thoughts. This was a fairly information packed section. Beginning to translate it to your real-time experience is where the value can start to be realized.

Section 4 | The Human Quotient - Practice & Profits

"People power is profit power…
power to the people!"

A Fantastic Twist to KPIs You'll Quickly Want to Use

The Human Quotient ™ In Practice

You've been learning about how the human experience impacts business. It's helped us develop a keen eye regarding human behavior from which we can quickly identify an issue and equally important, determine how to resolve it, *if it can* (in the context of a typical business setting).

As a reminder, we've coined this the "human quotient" and it's what's transferred to clients to help them more effectively work with the human aspects of their businesses... and this is what is sorely needed and dramatically missing among most business leaders and, as I've discovered over the years, their HR counterparts.

Without it, decision-making is greatly handicapped and many **decisions are made against the self-interest of the leader, employees and company goals.**

Here's an example.

In the HR, talent management world, we talk a lot about behavior competencies or the qualities desired in those we hire and company cultures. Yet, in many companies, those qualities are not emphasized, given much attention, or intentionally developed.

I think the main reason why is we don't understand or appreciate the direct impact qualities have (positive or negative) on our processes, results and profits.

In fact when you think about it, it's common for qualities to only be given significant attention when they are negative and have reached a level of *intolerance*. (Example: consistently late labeled as irresponsible vs. responsible. So, being irresponsible (being late) gets way more attention than being on time or being responsible.)

Imagine for a moment -- if there was a heightened, *intentional emphasis* on positive qualities – even qualities that would fuel a high-performance team. Imagine in a team or department those qualities being given lots of attention, talked about regularly, fostering collective awareness, support and reinforcement.

The result? I've seen over time those qualities *grow in volume, dimension and intensity,* even to the point of overcoming unwanted qualities. Additionally, they become fiercely protected because everyone is experiencing and enjoying their value.

And, if a new team member comes on the scene with negative qualities, one who - let's say is toxic - would have *difficulty fitting in* and perhaps wouldn't last very long *or* the collective power of the positive group qualities would influence a change in the behavior and performance of that team member. That's what I call "positive peer pressure".

> STOP FOR A MOMENT <

The last 3 paragraphs describes a profoundly different management practice! => Identify, focus, give attention to, reward, recognize positive qualities...not just behaviors common to typical performance management, but attributes, characteristics.

Imagine positive qualities being so pervasive, *in such volume,* so *deeply* characteristic (some call it the "DNA") of a company culture, that someone who behaves differently would feel uncomfortable and would either have to adapt or leave. *(refer to page 11)*

Practical Application - A Unique Twist to KPIs

KPIs are a common theme for measuring a variety of elements in business. As it relates to the theme of qualities, we encourage our clients to incorporate KPIs related to qualities. **We see positive qualities as a business asset** that should be *consistently tended to and measured*. We call them **"key people indicators".**

A great action=>Teams are encouraged to identify and *demonstrate* values and qualities they want their fellow team members to be possess and to which they've committed.

Those are regularly monitored. It's like taking the pulse of the team to monitor its health. **We see a team as healthy when its consistently emanating positive qualities.** If there is any variance, the reason is quickly discovered, taken seriously and appropriately addressed. Imagine addressing issues within a team quickly and effectively! Yeah!

One of the most significant shortcomings of many leaders is <u>not quickly addressing employee behavior issues</u>. (This harkens back to my earlier comment on tolerances).

It's clear to see that **qualities rule and they are fuel**! Certain qualities act as fuel, they give life, in fact are <u>*the energy of performance.*</u> We commonly call this being "empowered" – having power.

Certain qualities impact motivation, engagement and *provide strength* emotionally, physically and spiritually.

While some qualities empower, other qualities de-energize, can drain or suppress motivation, more specifically undermine one's life force. They are known as "disempowering".

Let's stop for a moment and make sure we're clear on what is a quality. Here's a simple dictionary definition:

Definition:
a distinctive attribute or characteristic possessed by someone or something.
"he shows strong leadership qualities"

Synonyms:
feature, trait, attribute, characteristic, point, aspect, facet, side, property
"her good qualities"

In the book Power vs. Force, here are some examples of qualities and their impact:

Energizing/empowering qualities: peace, joy, love, willingness, courage, acceptance, pride, desire, understanding, patience.

De-energizing/disempowering qualities: Fear (it can go either way initially, but sustained would trend toward depleting), grief, apathy, guilt, shame, despair, regret, despondence, discourage, pessimism. (Refer back to the side bar on "dissing" employees).

Important note: every human quality has a motivational and engagement quotient as well as a vibrational energy level that impacts an employee's experience, the atmosphere of a team and all the elements involved in human performance.

Example: I was on a team in my early professional life that had a team member that was habitually negative (what we would call today "toxic"). It was exhausting to be around him. Each team member spent energy either complaining about him or trying to avoid him. We were equally frustrated at what appeared to be our manager's inability or unwillingness to do anything about it.

Remember, when you look at the human chart, we as humans only have so much capacity and energy in a day to execute work. Some of that was taken up by this unhealthy team member. He was actually demotivating and "depressing" to be around. **The literal description…he "depressed" team members' energy level and motivation and disrupted focus** (was a distraction).

This is another example of why it's important to work for positive qualities in a team *as a business imperative* vs. just a nice thing to do.

Positive qualities produce profits.

This information, used over time and applied in real-time business situations, from what happens on the manufacturing floor to the c-suite, provides that needed **refined sensibility** to the human experience where:
> it becomes easier to detect,
> becomes easier to see the impact to the operations of a business,
> and therefore provides the motivation to quickly resolve the "human" issues of the operation.

That's why we can quickly save our clients' money while helping them make more – this is a unique, cultivated awareness and insight we bring.

Here's an example: working with a dysfunctional manager - by the way, if there has been one present for a period of time, you're already losing money - we can determine if that manager can be coached to improvement fairly quickly. If not, we give our clients the confidence and clarity to terminate and then help them hire or promote a better option that can quickly grow to operational effectiveness, supporting profitability.

Without this knowledge and awareness, dysfunctional managers are allowed to stay impairing results and getting paid for it! Think about this for a moment.

Keeping a dysfunctional leader is like paying someone to help you lose money.
Does this make sense? And yet, it's happening every day.

Qualities are the unavoidable components of what causes an employee, leader or business to be successful-- or not. And that's why it's critical that every leader and business owner sees and appraises their operations and performance of their employees in this way.

Qualities are a business building resource which every leader needs to embrace this.

Most leaders are conditioned to give attention to and emphasize performance (behaviors) over or instead of qualities. This is a missed opportunity.

For those *unattuned* to human energy, qualities and behavior, the typical leader or manager when assessing performance directs their attention towards an employee's presence and activity, not necessarily the qualities exhibited while present and active. Those matter too. Both impact the intended results and a company's P/L.

Example => Let's say you have a sales manager that directed his/her team to use specific tactics or processes known to get good results with clients. However, in the attempt to relay, teach and coach, team members are bullied, disrespected and threatened. Those leadership behaviors reflect qualities of aggression, perhaps an unhealthy ego, severe disrespect, impatient, hostility (probably more) and would certainly affect what could have been better results.

In fact, a proven formula or process could be weakened or seen as ineffective because of who and how it's being implemented.

Even a bad coach can ruin a good team.

Qualities Have Immediate, Short Term & Long Term Impact
All qualities at the outset have immediate impact for all those involved. Now imagine the impact, good or bad. Next, imagine that impact sustained over a period of time. It could generate a substantial effect – good or bad.

So, we have to see qualities not only as present, but also in terms of **intensity and duration** *and* who is being affected and for how long....all of which have financial repercussions. (We help clients create an impact map to sort this out).

Consider the operational impact with this in mind. Think for a moment about the positive quality of courage. Imagine it being present in the moment....now imagine it in huge doses, strengthen over a period of time, even bolstered through exceptional challenges and circumstances. It's safe to say, the results would be dramatic.

Now imagine a negative quality such as apathy being present in the moment. Now imagine it in larger doses over a period of time. What would be the impact to a team? Would anything get done? If nothing else, productivity would be low and its effect could easily spread like a heavy cloud...perhaps over an entire team encouraging other unhealthy, counterproductive behaviors to arise such as complaining, gossiping, or infighting... they could become dispirited, demotivated, disengaged....etc.

> The human qualities we possess and express have direct impact on *everything* we do -- in fact our very existence -- and so need to be seriously considered when leading and running a business.

Unfortunately, here's what I've discovered regarding a typical leader's relationship to qualities. *They are...*
- undervalued or not seen as valuable at all in the context of business operations
- their connection to achieving desired outcomes is not understood
- not emphasized enough
- seen as all or nothing vs. measure and dimension
- not understood as they relate to human behavior

As you have learned, it's to the advantage of every company that leaders at all levels learn how to see and understand the 'human' element of their business -- that is qualities, behavior and even energy.

Human Insight

The force of good can mute, suppress, *overcome* the force of bad.
Is there *enough* force of good within your teams? Force of good practically means qualities that feed, empower, enlarge, sustain the life force of each member such as...

Respect
Dignity
Trust
Fun
Enjoyment
Grace
Truth by way of Constructive Candor
Healthy Conflict
Emotional, Psychological, Physical, Spiritual Safety
Inspiration
Encouragement
Appreciation
Recognition
Caring
Humility
Personal maturity & responsibility

| Leadership Side Bar |

Human Behavior insight

Those who know me know that I have a deep passion to help. I hate to see people struggle unnecessarily! That's why I write, teach, coach and consult - to share my gift of insight.

This sharing requires candor. Used appropriately, candor can be a beautiful gift for periodic reality checks.

So, I'd like to share some candid truths about adult behavior. Use them as you will. I'm sharing them to serve your greatest good -- whatever your role.

1. Some people do not want to change and have no intention of doing so. With this truth, you must ask yourself, How do I need to use this information right now?"

2. Leaders frustrate themselves because they do not accept this...throw money at a "training" expecting a change that does not transpire. They "keep hope alive" while others suffer. This is a disservice to a team, a company and to the person who needs to change.

3. Without meaningful consequences, a behavior will continue.

4. Some employees, managers, and leaders genuinely don't care.

5. People fundamental change because "they" want to - not because you want them, expect them to or because they "should".

6. For those who don't want to, an external environment must be in place to mold a change, or so they or the behavior can no longer exist.

Broader View

Many leaders may think, "Well this is all fine and good, but I don't have the money to do these things." Or, "It doesn't matter how people are treated, my company still makes money."

In both cases I say, it's not so much how much are you making, but how much you are losing – what profits are being lost?

If you're losing profits it means you're having to work harder for the profits you do achieve, while addressing all the distracting "human resource" issues that take up time, energy and other resources.. all of which slow and bog down a business (I call them human bottlenecks).

Is that working and leading smart? *In reality many leaders create their own struggles and challenges – self-imposed - undermining the very results for which they work so hard.* Some then blame their employees and managers for the very conditions they've created.

What's the broader purpose and goal of your company and mission?

Many profitable companies could be so much more and with more ease if "the human quotient" was wholly integrated into a company's philosophy, practices and strategy. It's less stressful for all involved and incredibly satisfying.

A great place to work has a ripple effect to an immediate family, to close communities and ultimately to the global community at large.

Human Truth
'When it comes to successful people management & talent development, you'll either pay now or pay later.

A Specific View

One of the simplest ways to help clients understand the financial connection of the human quotient is with the following example:

Every human behavior expressed in a business context can be considered profitable, neutral or unprofitable.

For example: the behavior of being courteous positively touches the human spirit in a way that is motivating…it gives energy. In fact an act of kindness impacts brain chemistry that causes someone to feel good. Feeling good tends to feed energy.

Conversely if someone is cruel, the opposite effect occurs. Therefore, being cruel could be considered an unprofitable behavior because it diminishes, reduces the "human resource" of motivation.

Additionally, destructive behaviors are distracting. Employees end up having to use energy to deal with the effects, either individually or within groups.

Here, we've identified 2 *unprofitable behavior effects: demotivation and distraction.* Now consider the *frequency* and *degree* to which the behavior is expressed. The effect is now multiplied.

It is safe to say that when an employee or employees are not focused and motived you are losing money.

Here's why (and this is one of the measuring principles in the executive briefing Show Me the Money!), when you employee someone you assign a specific amount of compensation to expectations of their performance.

> *It is an investment* in their abilities, and all that they bring to bear to execute a job description contributing to the fulfillment of business objectives ,which produce revenue.
> We call this **"roc", return on compensation.**

You anticipate getting what you expect, which we call "at expected". When the employee performs at expected, you are achieving the exact *return on compensation* desired -- that you envisioned and identified when you hired them. "You do this and in exchange I'll pay you this."

If they perform more than expected, beyond their prescribed job description (and your expectation), their performance would be consider "above expected" and therefore, your return on investment (roc) would be higher.

If however, they perform below expected and even cause others to do so, that would be below expected. You would then be experiencing a loss of investment...multiplied.

Important Point => This is why quickly dealing with disruptive managers and employees or tightly coaching under-performance is not only a leadership and business management issue, but also a *financial strategy*.

It's also why annual performance reviews or appraisals alone are ineffective. Delaying needed feedback to adjust behavior and performance wastes money (this was mentioned in the conditioning section).

Regular feedback, successful coaching can turn under or at expected performance into above. Then, when someone requests a raise, they genuinely deserve it!

As mentioned, we help clients create *impact maps* to fully determine the effect certain behaviors have on various areas of the business. It's a useful practice you'll want to adopt.

The ability to see and quickly respond to employee performance issues at all levels of a company in *a fiscally responsible* way reflects "the human quotient" of a leader.

The quality of "good" in a business context is something that helps achieve desired outcomes; something positive in nature. The use of the word "positive' in business is used to describe measured or moving forward or in a direction of increase or progress.

The Human Quotient Measured & Financially Quantified
The Human Quotient View in Improving the Employee Experience

A Case Study

In our executive briefing *Show Me The Money! Solving the Mystery of ROI to Unlock Profits & Increase Company Value,* are multiple examples and an extensive explanation of how to calculate the financial impact of human behavior. Consider it human resource accounting 101 (without the algebra…phew!).

I thought it would be helpful to include one of my favorite examples that demonstrates what you've been reading.

Case Study | Department Turnaround Combined With Leadership Coaching - Manufacturing

Many of our clients have finally realized that traditional approaches (information dumps) to leadership-management training and development are not really working. Dr. Daniel Goleman, in his book *Working With Emotional Intelligence*, calls it "the billion dollar" mistake.

Unless it is with the specific intent to build knowledge, we discourage a one off, stand-alone seminar or workshop as a "solution" for skill and competency development.

Rather, we encourage them to experience spurts of learning combined with a **coaching intensive** (a customized, targeted learning experience for a fixed period of time with real-time embedded in real-time business operations with accountability). We conduct these both individually and with peer groups.

We start with assessing business needs and mindful of those results, initiate a launch session with the participants asking what areas they see / feel they need help. We connect those answers to the business needs for greater motivation and accountability, making the co-created development initiative more practical and *relevant*.

The initial needs list is called "W.I.I.F.M." (What's in it for me...what do we most want to get out of this). This approach helps them determine the personal benefits as well. They are fully participating in their own learning and co-created agenda for the experience.

Also of important note: This case study demonstrates that soft skill development *can be* measured.

Here's a list from the case study group:

Needs / Benefits of The Roundtable - Summary
Key Needs – Issues - Needs Improvement (as expressed by the group):
> Communication between departments
> Attitudes among team members & leaders
> How to get people motivated, dedicated
> How and what to prioritize
> Difficulty with supervisors
> How to give feedback, no rapport
> Better team work – be on the same page

Results After the 12 Week Roundtable
(as reported and experienced by the participants)

Leaders from Collaborating Departments:
- Created a better understanding of what each faced, generated empathy, caring and appreciation, adjusted expectations (e.g. knowing and understanding what's going on e.g. if manufacturing is shorthanded, the impact that has and how to respond supportively vs. suspicious or accusatory)
- Caused them to respond differently --- instead accusatory, blaming, which dragged down morale, discouraging and desire to help - gave benefit of doubt = doing their best, which improved relationships

- Rapport has improved across the board
- Helped to be on the same page between departments - this impacted communication - how and when

Specific Team/Department
- Communication - more respectful, understanding and collaborative without being defensive *activated desire* to help, volunteering to help
  - Before felt like being thrown under the bus during interdepartmental meetings, blaming via emails
- Responding more open-mindedly to inquiries and needs to "look, find, and fix" vs. trying to come up with excuses why it wasn't done or cannot be done (channeled thinking and energy to problem solving rather than excusing)
  - Better collaboration continued to build respect, trust and confidence between – everyone more approachable Improved productivity substantially
- Help generate more focus and desire to improve startup/downtime issue

Leadership Development

- Specific tactics implemented on how to increase shift productivity - to lead more effectively
- Building better rapport with each team member resulting in *improved responsiveness* to directives and team goals
- Significant increase in confidence in capability to lead a team
- Meeting in a group motivated leaders to see what was important to the director and needs of manufacturing
- Opened up communication=share more, inform more, trust

- Increased sense of pride and accountability due to sharing numbers with all stakeholders, quantitating contributions and achievements, challenges (also increased motivation)
- Hearing important issues from an outsider helped with leadership support
- Attitudes towards hourly team members changed vs. giving up on specific people - <u>demonstrated even a "trouble" employee can turn around and deliver substantial results</u> - this employee experienced 180 degree positive change - highly productive, using specialty skills
- Increased confidence in decision-making, capability to lead Impact in numbers in #'s, %, and/or $ (key areas reflecting significant return on investment).

Impact By the Numbers
Enhanced communication and rapport, sense of team collaboration, activating desire to problem solve and help via collective effort - address line 4 startup/downtime issue.
went from *3 hours downtime to 18 mins.*
94% efficient
$ recaptured = $2,375.00 per week - ripple impact $57,000 realized over 24 weeks.

Substantial increase in addressing maintenance notices
- Attained 100% completion in notifications - department record
- Consistent improvement each week
- Week 5 - 175 Notifications
- Weeks 12-19 19 / 34 done

Average costs
As of week 5 - average $11,000 per week (ranging $10,000 - $13,000) Average is down to average $3,000 per week (average recapture per week $8,000)

Simple savings calculation by weeks
5 - 8 average $11,000 x (4 weeks) = $44,000
9-12 average $3,000 x (4 weeks) - $12,000
$ recaptured impacting P/L in a 4 week period = $32,000 ($8,000 a week) Sustained over 24 weeks - $192,000

Additionally
1 Shift had its first ever record down day activity
Immediate financial / tangible impact during roundtable experience:
4 week #s: $9,500 - line 4
4 week #s $32,000 - downtown reduction In-house fabrication: $1,500
Initial Impact total - $43,000
Combined sustained 24 week impact: $249,000

Numbers not included but positively impacted:
> Increased return-on-investment for salary / hourly $ spent for needed performance - *team member performance at or above expectations*
> Retention of key team members (avoiding all related turnover costs including productivity and talent capabilities averages)

Summary
Impact considerations (just those reported - not included - related ripple effect not currently mapped): Conservative financial impact estimate - $250,000+

Roundtable and individual coaching seen as a "life preserver". The confidence developed within the team was the oxygen needed to infuse life into a team that was dying. See intangible list.

100% Return-on-investment achieved within first 2-3 weeks of engagement. 4-6 week ROI - 258%. ROI will continue to grow based on sustained practices.

This reflects the tangible process impact. Now let's look at the human (some might say intangible impact), which are equally important, causing the tangibles to occur.

Note: Though you many not completely understand what all the numbers represent, the most significant point is *there are numbers* and they are real. They represent the successful application of all the concepts – in this case – in a manufacturing environment.

Summary of Intangibles Lists

_ROI on hourly rate per team member increased due to substantial uptick in engagement (*meaning* enhanced connection, drive, desire, motivation = applied personal "human resource" to work) raising productivity. Several moved from below expected to at or above.

_*People started to care more because they felt cared for* -- getting attention and practical help...proved to themselves, things can get better. These things can work.

_Rise in engagement due to implementation of more *assertive, intentional leadership* coupled with group leadership techniques, which fostered consistent focus, goal achievement, bonding, sense of team, sense of value along with respectful accountability of individual contributions to expectations, creating continuity and community between all shifts. This increased confidence and sense of competence.

_Increased cross-departmental collaboration, increased respect and trust activating a desire to work together, problem solve, be helpful.

_Increased productivity cleared more time for strategic planning producing proactive activities, which helped mitigate machinery down time and available use of little used, but valuable skills for other needs.

To follow is the exact chart created by the team at the end of the coaching and peer roundtable experience. It's a very tangible case study **from the point of view of the participants.**

Notes:

Question: Viewing the chart to follow, how much value would you place on columns 1 & 2? How you identify *intangibles* for yourself? For your company?

INTANGIBLES		TANGIBLES
		#s, %, $
For Me	**For My Team**	**Immediate | Long Term**
Feeling more capable	Trust being built	*Several results reported, here are just a few:*
Confidence	Better problem solving	$1,500 saved /kept in house – fabrication need due to increased productivity, time available
Better attitude	More bonded	
Feel team is more confident in his leadership	Better rapport and respect	Manufacturing Line – 3 hrs of down time saved in a wk and each week after. Appx. $1,500 savings x 6 wks = $9,000 x 6 mths = $54,000
	Experiencing more efficiency in work	
Happy (hated coming to work, was going to step down)	More confidence	
	Better attitudes	Week 7 – 94% capacity – only 18 minutes of down time. Line start up savings appx./rounded down - $2,400.00 a week (sustained at same level) $2,400 x 24 weeks = $57,600
Feels appreciated	Significantly reduced 'shift competition and resentment"	
Better thought process	Sense of team work across all shifts = team cohesion	Just these 3 items – total savings for 6 months: $116,700.00
Gained specific techniques	Increased morale	
	More focused	*Ripple Effect or Impact Map Summary - Intangible to Tangible*
Relief – things are finally getting fixed	Better esteems	
Less stress	Communicating more and better	ROI on hourly rate per team member-increased due to substantial uptick in engagement (*meaning enhanced connection, drive, desire, motivation = applied personal "human resource" to work*) raising productivity.
More organized, better prioritizing	More time to be pro-active	
	Using, applying in-house talents to special projects vs. farming them out	
Getting more done		Rise in engagement due to implementation of more assertive, intentional leadership coupled with group leadership techniques, which fostered consistent focus, goal
Getting help	Better prioritizing	

Better communication "sees light at the end of the tunnel" Excited, hopeful Feels good about work and team Feel supported Decided to stay and not look for another position Less fearful of losing job	Greater sense of accomplishment Greater sense of contribution Increased quality of work Feeling more valued	achievement, bonding, sense of team, sense of value along with respectful accountability of individual contributions to expectations, continuity between all shifts. Increased productivity cleared more time for strategic planning producing proactive activities, which help mitigate machinery down time and available use of little used, but valuable skills for other needs

Notes

Now look at this chart and connect it to the elements of the human chart. This is what a successful leadership & management development initiative can look like. This also demonstrates how management development is organizational and business development.

This case study and our work suggests that for many leaders, what's holding back their business may not be what they think.

And here is where we can use the human quotient to assess what's happening. We've written this resource for this exact reason to be able to adequately assess-diagnose-prescribe the human aspect of their business. It's our twist on ADP. This is the power and value of definition #2 of the human quotient.

Leading and running a business can be a daunting endeavor no matter the size, even running a department or team for that matter can seem like a formidable challenge. The pressure is ever present to deliver results and for some, knowing how to improve results is the ultimate leadership test.

If you have not been getting the outcomes you want or wish to improve what's already a decent operation, there might be some "human elements" to consider that are undermining your business performance. *The human element or human experience is commonly overlooked in considering profitable improvements.*

It's not the first place many leaders and business owners consider and yet as you've been reading, it's clear this is an essential component to quickly improve results.

What's initially considered in the quest to enhance results is other resources and processes (sales & marketing, strategy & planning for example), rather than the "human resource".

This is not to say those areas should not be reviewed. It's just common that human performance is not in the mix or *weighted as a critical, contributing factor.*

We need to understand that **human performance is business performance management.** Successful business management must include talent/performance management.

And...it should start with the leader and or leadership team.

Even if human performance is considered, leaders don't typically *look at themselves first* and ask questions such as, "What about me and my leadership has allowed this to be or has lead us to where we are now or not?"

Even if you just need to fine tune your results, a careful look at the human experience within your operations would be useful. Here's a starter list of what to look for. You can apply this list to both you and your teams -- it would make a great "human point of view "operational assessment.

Qualities or conditions that impact human performance, undermine operational effectiveness and could ultimately be holding back your business...(starter list):
- confusion
- lack of clarity of what to do, or what is wanted
- saying yes too much
- not saying no enough
- overwhelm
- fear
- out of control ego
- lack of process (the tangible, executable road map)
- lack of courage
- not communicating frequently enough
- lack of trust
- broken rapport with team members
- not communicating clearly
- keeping and/or not addressing toxic employees
- inability to prioritize
- pushing too hard
- pushing too little
- leadership vacuum
- lack of boundaries
- discouragement
- lack of relevant knowledge
- unresolved hurts
- arrogance
- minimal appreciation
- micro-managing
- disrespect
- lack of focus
- absence of accountability

As you review the list, give thought to these questions:

1> How does this list related to the human chart?

2> Do you truly believe addressing any of these will impact your profits?" I ask that, because though many leaders say yes to that question, *they don't act or make decisions in a way that reflects that belief.* This is a sure indicator they really don't believe it. **Actions reflect beliefs and inaction reflects beliefs.**

For example, if you as a leader have struggled with any of these for an extended period time and have not gotten help, that suggests there is a belief (probably subconscious) that it's not important, it doesn't matter and it's really not relevant to the bigger picture -- *that it's not affecting the business outcomes or revenue.*

As has been our running theme through-out this read, **many leaders function with a perilous insensitivity to how the human experience in their company environments impacts business outcomes**. This is a leadership hazard that must be remedied. Without doing so, the human resource of a company will be perpetually misused and under-utilized. (*Side note:* some would place this type of sensitivity under the umbrella of emotional intelligence.)

This insensitivity can be costly!

In my experience getting help and effectively addressing the items on the list don't have to be a full-blown science experiment. Perhaps seeing it as such is what holds back decision-makers from seeking assistance.

Leadership Reflection: Great question to ask any employee… at any level, "What am I missing?" What am I not seeing?" Tip: Voluntarily fill your blind spot

Bottlenecks Matter!

It's not a sophisticated business or management term, yet it's happening every day in organizations everywhere.

I'm confident in saying that if someone asked a leader, "What's holding back your business?", the items on the list suggested above would probably not be mentioned or top of mind and yet even one of these effectively addressed could unlock better outcomes and profits.

Additionally, any one of these on the list can create what I call "human bottlenecks". Where ever there is a bottleneck there is a slow done or halt to the execution of business operations and strategy. And left unattended can adversely affect talent.

Bottleneck examples:
> 2 leaders do not trust each other, critical information sharing may not be occurring.
>A manager can be deemed ineffectual if there is such a breach in respect, team members refuse to be sufficiently responsive to requests or directives.
> 2 teams members locked in a relentless personality conflict, long held resentments or unresolved disagreement.

Why are the human bottlenecks in your team or organization? How is not addressing them affecting the business?

Human bottlenecks undermine and delay revenue.

And Just When You Think I've Gotten Too "Woo Woo" On You

Here's where is all comes together. THE most powerful leadership development combination is the human element integrated into a results-based format, combined with strategy, embedded in daily business operations.

The duration of my time spent in management and leadership development has netted a format that predictably and meaningfully gets results that can be measured. We call it **"results-based" leadership**. It provides a framework from which any company can work to improve their leaders' competencies and to which proprietary strategy and processes can be applied.

I referenced earlier the need for companies to install a *leadership & management infrastructure*. This format does just that. It speaks to many needs in the marketplace. *Here's what I mean.*

I start every leadership group coaching session with these two questions:
- ✓ What is leadership?
- ✓ What's the point of it?

Those questions usually generate looks of confusion, blank stares and the painful expression of "why are you asking that?"

Many in my coaching groups have been leaders for years – they are generally not newbies and yet have difficulty answering the questions.

Do you find it curious that those who've been leaders for years cannot quickly and precisely articulate what their title represents or what role they've been playing…or how they meaningfully contribute to the business?

Here's what I've discovered, the lack of precision and specifics, as well as a *deficit of leaders who can competently lead and train other leaders,* has muddled the would be success and effectiveness of many *(and here is another compelling reason for effective leadership training).*

If you were to strip down all of the discussion about leadership and extract all information and wisdom from the thousands of books written about it, you could draw one simple conclusion: the point of being a leader is to get *needed* results.

In the context of business that can also be translated into being a meaningful business partner -- providing a return on investment utilizing available resource for agreed compensation.

Sounds simple enough right? Well it's simple only if there is a tangible, measurable way to accomplish it.

So I've made it my mission to create a tangible framework that when utilized creates an undeniable leadership contribution -- one characterized by consistently achieving substantial results.

I've named the framework "results-based leadership", which sounds a bit redundant when you think about. But I purposely use this phrase to make the distinction that leaders exist to get desired, needed outcomes, not just to be present or busy…or to create chaos and dysfunction.

Here is an introduction to our results-based leadership framework which we've consolidated into our 5 Step Predictive System.

1. Identify the results – what do you want and expect? Be clear, targeted and specific. This is commonly known as create a vision. But I don't want to use that term because I think that sounds vague.

2. Have daily targets – translate those results into daily targets. It utilizes a key performance management principle, "tight accountability equals higher performance."

3. Consistently (daily, frequently) communicate expected results, in constructive, creative, coaching/teaching, positive, inspiring, motivating ways. The key tip -- communicate verbally and visually.

4. Hold team members accountable - continually lead and coach to outcomes.

Here's where style really matters. The way in which accountability is conducted can be used to harness and fuel motivation, nurture engagement, fine tune focus, develop capabilities while fostering trust, respect, appreciation, and sense of value.

5. Consistently assess results within targeted time frames. If desired results are not occurring, leaders need to know why and address the deficit in a *timely manner*. It's amazing what can be discovered about process and people when keen attention is paid to why results are or are not being met within a certain time span.

6. Coach the gaps - provide feedback in a way that teaches and trains for improved performance. This is where alignment occurs – it's when leaders take the opportunity to identify behaviors needed, matching them to actions and/or processes to increase the probability of hitting the mark.

7. For as much as you can, measure, track, share results in #, %, $. There's a big difference in the psychology of motivation when specific metrics or measurements are used to define achievement. Here's an example:
    - "Congratulations team, we've improved production this week."
    - "Congratulations team, We've improved production 25% over last week."
    - "Congratulations team, our production went from 50% to 75% in just 2 weeks.

   Which statement(s) has the greater impact?

8. Celebrate – it's a motivator and reinforcement of the behavior and outcomes you want more and more of.... reward, recognize, show appreciation.

Now, the style in which these elements are executed matter – a collaborative coaching style that is "human-centered" is an essential ingredient to successful implementation. A dictatorial, oppressive style will have an adverse effect. So in our system, we've included performance pillars that reflect the appropriate qualities to achieve the best results.

With this practical approach, you and your leaders can use this map to improve their performance. If they are not getting results, you can find something within this framework/system to improve the probably they will.

It can address needs from both an executive leadership and human resource perspective. Tested within a variety of leadership challenges, it has proven to provide extraordinary success!

In summary, we have a human-centered, results-based leadership system that has been successfully tested in a variety of settings – from millennial to legacy leaders.

"The challenge of leadership is to be strong, but not rude; be kind, but not weak; be bold, but not bully; be thoughtful, but not lazy; be humble, but not timid; be proud, but not arrogant; have humor, but without folly."
– Jim Rohn

Section 5 | Summary Information

"My experience leading people has taught me that employees want to do meaningful work in a place where they can have an extraordinary sense of community, a place that has high standards, a place that cares about them as individuals, and a place where they can learn and grow."
@Doug Conant | Founder & CEO, Conant Leadership, Former President Nabisco Foods; Former CEO Campbell Soup

In Summary...
here are my critical observations and insights from those trips around the block *(20 years' worth)*:

- Everything about the success of an organization begins and ends with its leaders and how they create and facilitate the human experience through their company culture.

- Leaders have great intentions yet have blind spots related to this truth because much of this truth is related to human behavior, not necessarily process or strategy.

- Many are afraid to appear weak or inadequate and therefore don't seek help when needed.

- There is a great albeit legitimate fear of wasting money to get help. Yet, that hesitation leads to decisions that in fact do exactly that - waste money. *(pay now or pay later... you are always paying in some way).*

- The sooner leaders get help – the faster their company grows.

- Many HR professionals are expert at administrative functions but know little about how human behavior or talent development impacts business results.

- For those that do, they may not be seen or treated as meaningful business partners.

- Most leaders do not see talent & human resource management as business management. Yet it directly impacts the P&L and company growth.

- "Training" must be seen as an investment vs. cost...seen as investing in building a business foundation and infrastructure, and high-performing culture.

- Many leaders do not understand the concept of company culture and the substantial impact it's having on the P&L.

- Many managers are not held to achieving results and being *fiscally responsible* in doing so.

It's because of the above that we offer what we do, help in the way we do…and from which we've crafted our mission…and which sets us uniquely apart.

> Jot down your key take-aways here…

What I Wish Every Manager Knew
A Knowledge Point Assessment

"You do not know what you do not know and you cannot change what you do not see."

There are 45 so far. Consider this a list by which to build your knowledge base of those of your leadership team at every level. I consider this list essential to being an effective, competent manager.

1. Who they are on the inside determines what kind of manager they are on the outside
2. Their natural leadership style
3. That their relationship with their staff (how they treat people) is the number one influencer in the performance of each team member.
4. How people operate
5. Natural wiring (personality type)
6. How the brain works
7. What motivates humans
8. Emotional maturity matters and is the number 1 reason for disruptive employees
9. Measuring is key to getting desired results (Note: everybody get results…they just may not be the ones you want.)
10. Effective performance mgt. …what that looks like
11. How people develop
12. How to be an effective coach
13. How to build and nurture collaboration
14. Effective leaders are able to look at themselves honestly (not afraid of self-reflection)
15. Effective leaders are comfortable in their own skin
16. How to effectively lead a group/team (leverage peer pressure for increased productivity)
17. Difference between a job description and a job competency (or critical success factor)

18. It's all about execution and the ability to get outcomes
19. How generations impact individual behavior
20. How to be respectful – practically
21. Slight edge matters – it's little things done consistently that goes along way
22. Adequate knowledge of technology DOES increase productivity
23. Consistent success is based in habits.
24. Managing their own careers, helps and empowers them to be better managers
25. That it's all about managing self, people, process, things, information and stuff to get better results.
26. Know when to let someone go
27. Know that keeping a disruptive, toxic team member undermines their leadership, motivation and productivity of a team and the financial bottom line of a company.
28. Learning how to think creatively for self and team is an essential skill.
29. Got to train their team how to think.
30. Creating/ nurturing team culture actually makes their job easier.
31. Hierarchy leadership in teams is an old school model
32. Most leaders use only a very small percentage of their team's potential
33. How to use the concept of a staff meeting more effectively to develop skills and leadership, train, hold people accountable, increase results, and improve processes with best practices.
34. Hire beyond the job description
35. Be People Wise – know who is safe and who is not
36. Learn how to read people more effectively
37. That the real "trainers" of an organization are not the official trainers, but the managers and supervisors (those who oversee that daily performance of employees).
38. Identifying and understanding job functions, skills, etc.
39. Personal Power is essential to the effective use of Positional Power

40. The concepts of "writing people up", exerting "discipline" is old school, command and control leadership concepts. Coach up or coach out is new school.
41. That tight accountability equals higher performance.
42. That without a meaningful consequence most behavior will not change.
43. That the lack of EQ or emotional intelligence is THE most significant contributor to underperforming and disruptive employees.
44. That everyone has a preferred work orientation towards people, task, and information.
45. That personal power trumps positional power every single time

In Conclusion

The intent of this writing is to stir your thinking, to spark a discussion among leadership teams regarding how to practically improve results by developing their human quotient.

This information begins to fill a critical knowledge gap most leaders and business owners possess and which sorely needs to be filled.

We recommend starting a discussion about the concepts in this briefing. We're happy to facilitate one for you in greater detail through our Leadership Roundtables, which we conduct both virtually or in person – at your next event or leadership retreat. We have a workbook that guides the discussion and can be used to craft an improvement plan.

Imagine the financial impact of fully incorporating the human truths we brought to your attention.

We offer complimentary discussions via phone or video conference – if you'd like to talk through how this applies to your organization. So don't hesitate to connect with comments or questions.

Additional copies of this briefing can be requested at a discount.

Wishing you mad success!
       JoAnn Corley-Schwarzkopf
       Executive Advisor
       Strategic Business Management Consultant
       Helping leaders successfully integrate talent management with business management and growth
       888.388.0565

www.jcsbusinessadvisors.com

~ An Invitation to Work With Us ~

If you're like our clients, they are busy leaders. So they opt to get help to make needed improvements and to quickly experience the their benefits.

We can save you time and money while accelerating results.

Because of our expertise in connecting human behavior to optimizing operations and better business outcomes, we've created a system that incorporates "human performance technology" (hpt) that you can use to rapidly achieve meaningful outcomes rather than going it slow and alone.

Our mantra: Borrow our expertise until you acquire your own.

We can do a needs assessment and help you implement a plan that's embedded in your day to day operation. We can help you quickly improve with minimal disruption at any level of assistance you're comfortable.

Check out our *5 Step Predictive System for High-Performance*. It creates a powerful infrastructure to cultivate the needed behaviors-performance of your leaders, managers and individual contributors, fosters a positive, productive high-performing culture, while continuing to generate revenue. It's business building, talent and operational management all in one.

Or, *bring this topic to your next leadership meeting.*

Email or call us today…we can schedule an "I'm curious, let's talk" session.

joann@jcsbuinessadvisors.com | 888.388.0565

| MORE ABOUT JOANN CORLEY-SCHWARZKOPF |

2017 CHAIR: CHIEF TALENT OFFICER EXCHANGE – CHICAGO
PANELISTS: CTO-GAP BRANDS, FANNIE MAE, FRONTIER COMMUNICATIONS

|> PROFESSIONAL RECOGNITIONS & HIGHLIGHTS
2012 - One of the first North American Career Advice Contributors for the Daily Telegraph UK
2013 - Open Sesame - Top 50 HR Professionals to Follow
2013 - Top 100 Social HR Experts 2013- Huffington Post
2015 - Top 100 Most Influential People in Human Resources & Recruiting
2015 - Top 100 Management Experts to follow on Twitter
2015 - Invited to be an IBM Futurist-Influencer
2016 - Top 100 Management Experts to follow on Twitter
2017 - Top 300 Women in HR Technology
2017 - Top 50 Unstoppable Women in HR
2017 - Top 100 Octoleader
[What makes an #OctoLeader? It is the way they leverage their personal brands to build professional communities of shared interest. It is the way they amplify their brand's platform through increased reach and engagement. It is the example they set as marketing leaders by sharing helpful content and daring to challenge the status quo.]
2017 - Chair, Chief Talent Officer Exchange, Chicago
2017 - Atlanta Voyager Magazine: Up & Coming
2017 Invited to partner with LinkedIn Learning as a subject matter expert to produce HR & Management courses

2018 – Expanded brand & name change from The Human Sphere to JCS Business Advisors
2018 – Global 500 Top Female HR Speakers
2018 – Top 30 Global HR Influencers
2018 – 50 Unstoppable Women in HR Tech
2018 – Invited to be on the board of the Global Women's Economic Forum

|> IN THE MEDIA

I've had the opportunity for lots of media experience. It's been fun! From being quoted by NBC News and the Harvard Business Review and industry publications like SHRM and ATD to being featured as a radio guest and on-line articles. And the highlight was being on the same radio show as Josh Gordy, a member of the super bowl winning Green Bay Packers. I got to hold "the ring"!

|> AUTHORSHIP

Amazon Author Page: https://www.amazon.com/JoAnn-R.-Corley/e/B004HGQKZ2

Show Me the Money! Solving the Mystery of ROI to Unlock Profits & Increase Company Value.

15 Shifts - The Essential Guide to Transform Your Talent Management

The 1% Edge - Power Strategies to Increase Your Management Effectiveness

Organizational Strategies for the Overwhelmed: How to manage your time, space, & priorities to work smart, get results, and be happy

Brain on Fire - Unleashing Your Creative Superpowers

Working Wisdom – A Journal

The Force Within

Ordinary Women, Extraordinary Success – contributing author (a collaborative effort with some of the top female motivational speakers in North American and hailed by Jack Canfield of Chicken Soup for the Soul fame as a must read.)

|> AROUND THE WEB

Em: joann@jcsbusinessadvisors.com

Website: www.jcsbusinessadvisors.com

Blog: www.joanncorleyspeaks.com

Phone: 888.388.0565

Skype: joann.corley

Twitter: @joanncorley | Also: LinkedIn, Google+, Pinterest, Instagram

Facebook: Professional page link:
https://www.facebook.com/joanncorley.thehumansphere

Amazon author page: https://www.amazon.com/JoAnn-R.-Corley/e/B004HGQKZ2

YouTube:
https://www.youtube.com/channel/UCtDQBHSnETZ5FIvThbx5oBA

iTunes: https://itunes.apple.com/us/podcast/joann-corleys-the-human-sphere-podchats/id519849819

Soundcloud: https://soundcloud.com/joann-corley-1

Medium: https://medium.com/@joanncorley

www.ingramcontent.com/pod-product-compliance
Lightning Source LLC
Chambersburg PA
CBHW071404220526
45469CB00004B/1158